BREAKING THE ADOLESCENT CODE

10 TRUTHS PARENTS SHOULD *KNOW*

10 THINGS PARENTS SHOULD *DO*

10 TRAPS PARENTS SHOULD *AVOID*

By

MATTHEW DUGGAN, PH.D.

www.drdugganandassociates.com

Breaking the Adolescent Code

By Matthew Duggan, Ph.D.

4137 E. 7th St., Long Beach, CA 90804

All rights reserved. No part of this book may be reproduced or transmitted in any form or by any means, electronic or mechanical without the author's permission.

ISBN 0-9839281-1-9

COPYRIGHT © 2012

Printed in the United States of America

DEDICATION

This book is dedicated to my parents Matthew and Mary Jane Duggan. Their love provided me with the courage to dream, their support with the confidence to reach for those dreams, and their patience with the ability to learn from my many mistakes in pursuit of those dreams. I am forever their son and proud of it.

And to my wife Kristina who is not only my best friend but also the rock of my life. Parenting with you is not a task but a joy.

Lastly to my daughter Shannon and my son Matthew IV who have taught me there is no greater gift in the world than to be called Dad.

CONTENTS

INTRODUCTION   1

THE BASICS

Chapter 1	Parental Sanity Check	8
Chapter 2	Be in Control of Your Own Thoughts and Mood	13

- The Subconscious
- All or None Statements
- Happiness/Positivism
- Perspective

Chapter 3	The Five Myths of Psychotherapy	22

- Myth 1: People who enter psychotherapy are crazy.
- Myth 2: Therapy is painful.
- Myth 3: The therapist tells you what to do and things get better.
- Myth 4: If I go to a psychologist, it means I can't solve my own problems.
- Myth 5: You have to have a major problem before you consult a psychologist.

10 TRUTHS PARENTS SHOULD KNOW

Chapter 1	Kids Want Good Lives	27
Chapter 2	How Did My Kid Know That?	31
Chapter 3	The Many Faces of Maturity	36
Chapter 4	The Holy Grail of Adolescence – The Pleasure and Pain Principle	40
Chapter 5	How You Say It Often Matters More Than What You Say ▪ Resiliency Theory	44
Chapter 6	Frames Are Everything	52
Chapter 7	Understand Your Power (Your Reactions and What They Mean) ▪ Be Wise with House Rules ▪ Deal Breakers ▪ Teaching vs. Berating ▪ Learned Helplessness	60
Chapter 8	Building a Home Contract: 15 Hot Tips	71
Chapter 9	What Makes a Kid Successful: EQ Over IQ	82
Chapter 10	What if Your Adolescent Has a Severe Psychiatric Issue?	88

10 THINGS PARENTS SHOULD DO

Chapter 1	Listen…..and They Will Tell You Exactly Who They Are	93
	- Listening	
	- Respecting	
	- Bridging Statements	
	- Listening Moments vs. Teaching Moments	
Chapter 2	The Three C's – Create a Culture of Communication	101
Chapter 3	Open Tough Subjects…and Wait for That Silence	108
Chapter 4	Understand, Empathize, and Above All Discipline	112
	- But it's Not Fair	
	- Support is More Important than Fairness	
	- Practicality Trumps Theory	
	- I Need My Kids to Agree with Me	
	- No Need to Argue With Kids	
Chapter 5	Make Adolescents Responsible for Their Own Behavior	122
	- Pendulum Rewards and Consequences	
	- Organize – Don't Moralize	
Chapter 6	Have Fun	130
	- Nicknames	
	- Metaphors and Analogies	
Chapter 7	Find Niches, Build Niches, Use Niches (It's All About Niches)	142
	- Building on a Niche	
Chapter 8	Risk Taking Can Be Good	147
Chapter 9	All Roads Start with the Good	152
	- Build on the Good	
	- Catch them Being Good	
Chapter 10	Be a Leader	156

10 TRAPS PARENTS SHOULD AVOID

Chapter 1	How to Raise a Teenzilla	162
Chapter 2	Adolescent See – Adolescent Do: What You Do is Worth So Much More Than What You Say	167
Chapter 3	Your Adolescent Has Enough Friends – Be a Parent	172
Chapter 4	The Kid's Dictionary: Teaching Your Kids the Meaning of Words	179
Chapter 5	Let's Torture Ourselves: Replaying the Past to Heal Old Wounds	184
Chapter 6	What Rules You? Thinking vs. Feeling	189
Chapter 7	Five Stressors That Will Really Cost You • Nasty Divorces • Teenage Parenthood • Absent Fathers • A Psychiatrically Ill Parent • Homework	193
Chapter 8	Loving a Child Into a Handicap • Marshmallow Mom and Popsicle Dad • Learning to Fail	199
Chapter 9	Stop Talking to Your Adolescent • Saying Less is More • Don't Tell Kids What They Already Know	207
Chapter 10	If You Want Privacy and Equal Rights – Buy a House • Privacy • Voting Rights • Trust and Verify	211

Epilogue 216

INTRODUCTION

You know what really irritates me? PSYCHOBABBLE! You know what I mean. It is the kind of advice I read in 'sophisticated' texts geared toward 'understanding the human psyche and its intricate mechanisms'. It is the junk you hear from the talking heads on television and radio when they do not know an answer and so decide to confuse the viewers with Psychobabble (commonly referred to as BS in most other circles). It is the kind of convoluted advice which takes you ten minutes to digest and often far less time to purge. That is NOT what you will find in this book.

This book is about straight-forward talk aimed at helping you to better understand your adolescent and be the best parent you can be. What I have found in my 25 years of treating children, adolescents and families is that almost every parent wants to be the best parent they can be. However, all of a sudden, you may find that you do not understand this creature in front of you. Where is that cute little ten year-old girl who used to jump into Daddy's arms each night before bed? Where is that funny little 8 year-old boy who could not wait to get out of bed in the morning to start the day?

The good news is they are still there, right in front of you – it's just that they have changed a bit and understanding them will provide you with the keys to making the transition from childhood to adulthood much more enjoyable for both of you.

I will use the term '"raise" your adolescent because you are still doing that regardless of how it feels right now. This is not just a transition time for your child but for you as well. I laugh when people talk about "parenting" as if it is one single skill instead of a constantly changing mosaic, which requires different skill sets at different developmental levels. Just look at your behaviors with your child between the ages of birth and 2, compared with 13 – 16. The way you parent is totally different.

    I saw a great interview with a man who ran the Boston Marathon in his mid-eighties. They asked him, "What is the best part of growing older". He said, "Growing"! That's what parenting is, an ever evolving skill set which is constantly growing. You don't have all the answers and neither do I. However, it is NEVER too late to pick up some useful skills in order to sharpen our parenting skills. I not only want kids to learn and grow, I want parents too as well. Hopefully, no matter what your current skill set, or whether you have a 6 year-old or a 16 year-old, this book can provide you with some useful skills to place in your 'parenting arsenal'.

    I think this is why adolescence comes when it does. You have done a lot of parenting up until now. You have learned a lot since the day they handed you this lovable bundle of joy and tossed you out of the hospital. Adolescence is when all this learning culminates and you step up your game.

    Like your adolescent, you are assuming more responsibility. And like him, when you accept more responsibility the rewards become bigger and more profound, i.e., watching your child mature, seeing him graduate, watching him develop long-term relationships and all the rest of the adventures that come as your child grows into a young man or woman. Although these years may provide some hurdles, they will fade away as you watch your son or daughter become a full functioning, well rounded, adult.

    So why should you listen to what I have to say? I have been treating children, adolescents and families for almost twenty-five years. I have worked in almost every setting imaginable, from running an adolescent psychiatric unit at a major medical center, to supervising an adolescent drug unit, to being elected to a Board of Education and helping run a school district, to running my own private practice (with 9 associates working in it) for the past 20 years. While I treat children and adults as well, the one constant throughout my training and experience has been my appreciation (and fascination) of adolescents and their families.

Adolescence can mean many things. Often adolescents are described as out of control, narcissistic entities who will do whatever they want whenever they want. While this may be true, they are also children becoming young adults. It is important to realize that they are not formed yet. They are not mini-adults nor are they static creatures doomed to remain what you may see in front of you. Just as clay can appear lumpy and misshapen before it is shaped by a craftsman, adolescents may look chaotic and uncontrolled prior to becoming mature adults. Adolescents will make many mistakes along the way (as I imagine each one of us can remember from our own adolescence). On the bright side they are often free spirits, creative thinkers and people who see the world in a novel way. They can be quite emotional and their way of looking at the world is often unique and fascinating.

Before going any further I would like to discuss three concepts which I have found are almost universally true:

1. The first is that parents love their children. I know this sounds strange to assert but I am often asked in public forums what the parents are like of the kids who see me. Don't you just have to love a kid and they will turn out OK? My answer is the parents of the kids I see are just like you and me. They love their kids deeply. Think about it; these parents must REALLY love their kids if they are spending all this time and effort to make sure their child is happy. I call the families that see me the top "5 percenters". These families have two things that make them special – the insight to realize something is wrong, and the guts to do something about it. It is no wonder I have so much deep respect for the people I see. I am fortunate to be able to work with people who possess these attributes.

2. People want to know if the parents are to blame for their kid's problems. This one is slightly trickier to address because often there

is some parental involvement at issue but it is not the whole picture. I can tell you that it is a good day, maybe even a great day, when a parent is entirely responsible for their adolescent's problem. I mean talk about shooting fish in a barrel. Parents will change in a split second if I tell them their child will benefit. It's a much tougher day when I have to tell parents that they cannot make the changes which are necessary to help their child. Then we are talking about a tough hill to climb where the parents can only marginally help because the problem resides within the child and he must make the change. It is not uncommon for me to hear a parent say, "Please tell me I am the problem! I will change today". It is my hope that this book will help parents recognize the changes they can make to be better parents.

3. Almost every single adolescent I have ever seen wants a better life. That is why they are doing what they are doing. They are trying (in their adolescent ways) to improve their lives. Whether it is taking drugs, disobeying, lying, etc. – they think this will make their life better. I know it seems hard to comprehend when a kid does something uniquely foolish, that in his way of thinking this was supposed to increase the value of his life. However, if you think about it this way, you will be in a far more powerful position to discuss it with him and come up with better ways to deal with the current problem.

As you read this book I would like you to keep a few things in mind:

1. I will be using the words he and she as they relate to each story. However, instead of writing he/she throughout this text, the default pronoun will be masculine. While some issues are more prominent in boys and others in girls, this book is about sharing knowledge and tools that can be used with either gender.

2. Most of this book is geared toward helping parents understand and help their children grow successfully through adolescence. However, I am well aware (and you should be too) that many of the

principles outlined in this book are best started when your child is younger. For instance, in a chapter like 'The Three C's: Create a Culture of Communication', it should be obvious that you will have better communication with your adolescent if this is started at a younger age. However, please remember, it is NEVER too late to start improving communication with your child. Throughout the book I will use the words adolescent, child and kid interchangeably. When I want to focus just on pre-teens I will state that in the reading. Therefore do not get too concerned about the nouns used.

3. My suggestion is you think of your own child/adolescent and use him as you are visualizing what you are reading. I realize there are a variety of family circumstances that make parenting more difficult. I have worked with almost every configuration of family conceivable. Whether you are a single parent, a stepparent, someone taking in foster children, a traditional two parent family, etc., all of these concepts still apply. Being a better parent means that you work to improve on what your current situation is. Again, no parent is perfect and no situation is perfect. The best you can do is your best. Go for it.

4. The book is designed for you to be able to skip around and read the chapters that you find to be the most authentic to your experience. Each of the chapter's stands on its own and can be read and used without knowledge of what came before it or after it. Some chapters fit together nicely and appear together (for instance, 'Listen….and They Will Tell You Exactly Who They Are', 'The Three C's: Create a Culture of Communication' and 'Open Tough Subjects' are variants on the same theme – communicating with your adolescent). If you run across a chapter, which does not seem to fit with your circumstances, just skip it and go to one that does. As with raising adolescents, there is no single right way to read the book. Use it as a reference or guide, and view the ideas as a smorgasbord from which you can pick and choose.

5. When you read the table of contents you will see the book is broken down into 4 sections. The first focuses on some

FOUNDATIONAL IDEAS that are important for all parents raising an adolescent. The second section outlines things I think you should KNOW about adolescents. The third focuses on things you can DO to help your adolescent. The last focuses on the TRAPS I see parents fall into which should be avoided.

6. Lastly, I use many examples in the book. Some are actual stories from my experiences and some are a combination of various cases. I have changed any identifying data to disguise the actual cases leaving intact the meaning to be gleaned from the example. Confidentiality is important in our field and it is always respected.

Given these premises and suggestions, my hope is that you will find in this book useful ways you can help your adolescent grow into adulthood.

THE BASICS

CHAPTERS 1 - 3

CHAPTER 1

PARENTAL SANITY CHECK!!!

If you are going to read only one chapter in this book, this would be the one. This is so fundamental I am putting it ahead of all the knowledge and tools and traps I will describe. If this one is not done, the rest of the tools will be useless. It is crucial that ALL PARENTS, WHO WANT TO BE BETTER PARENTS, MAKE SURE THEY ARE EMOTIONALLY NOURISHED SO THEY CAN GIVE BACK TO THEIR CHILDREN.

Every time you are on a plane the flight attendant says "in the event that the masks deploy, make sure your mask is secure before helping others". That is the golden rule in parenting. You cannot be a good parent if you are stressed out, over-worked and not taking care of your own basic needs.

Some years back I was giving a talk to a group of parents. I was talking about having fun with your kids and suddenly a younger mom raised her hand. I called on her and she said, "You know Doctor, sometimes I just want to run away from my kids". This comment was well off topic. As I was thinking about what to say a peculiar thing happened. The audience began to clap for her. She had hit a nerve, and an important one at that. What initially she had been afraid to say for fear of sounding like a bad parent really resonated with every parent in the place. This was before I had kids so I could relate a little. Now I have two and I should have been clapping too. There are just times that no matter how much you love those little rug rats, they just drive you crazy. Multiply this by about a million and you can see how frustrated parents can become with adolescents.

Throughout this book, I will be discussing a lot of topics and describing numerous tools. Some will resonate with you and some will not. But keep in mind one important thing - you must keep yourself in good psychological/emotional shape in order to be a good parent. I do not know any good parent who is bedraggled, constantly spent, and out of emotional energy. Kids sense this and react to this. If you are always stressed out, depressed, giving too much, then you will inevitably not be able to raise your kids in a healthy manner.

One important component, which affects adolescents, but is most determinative of the emotional state of younger children, is your own emotional state. Most younger children do not know how to feel about experiences so they watch you to see what your reaction is and then they adopt it. For instance, if your child says they are scared of the boogieman, they are testing you to see if YOU are scared of the boogieman. If you run around with your head in your hands yelling "Oh no, not the boogieman", you have verified to your child that he should be afraid. If you react with love, support and reassurance that you are not afraid, and neither should he be, his emotions will change quite quickly. This is one of the reasons when I hear about a young child being depressed or anxious I always assess the parent, who is usually either depressed or anxious and passing this onto their own child, who then shows the emotion. It is a good prognostic indicator that the child is not really depressed or anxious but just responding to the parent's emotional state. This again shows how important it is for each parent to take care of his or her own emotional needs. It makes a gigantic difference in how successful you will be as a parent.

This is why I always start therapy with one of my adages, TAKE CARE OF YOURSELF FIRST and then you will be able to take care of your kids. Ironically, this means spending more time with yourself and less with your kids. That's right, I said it. <u>Spend more time on you and less on your kids.</u> This will assure that during the time you spend with them they will have a fully competent, emotionally available mom and dad, not someone who desires to run from them all the time. Even then, there will be times you need to run – do it (Note: Do not take this too literally and leave your children in a restaurant, mall or other public setting. This could lead to much bigger problems than feeling run down that day). Make sure your batteries are charged otherwise you are useless. I cannot tell you the number of parents I meet who are so over-spent taking their kids to events, school, homework, etc., that they have nothing left to give their kids when it is vital – when they are approachable.

I often tell overspent parents they need to join a tennis league, a bowling team, etc. They ask, "How can I fit it in"? EXACTLY. This should be a top priority for each parent. And this goes double for time spent with your husband or wife. Never place your spouse behind your children. The foundation of any family is the marital relationship. If this is weak or flawed you can expect a bumpy ride through child rearing. This is why there should always be Mommy and Daddy time where the kids know the parents are not to be disturbed. When I grew up our signal to leave Mom and Dad alone was their shutting the door to their room. If we knocked, and it was not vital, we were punished (Good idea). The stronger the bond between parents the more it leaks down to the kids. My parents have been married over 50 years. Do you think my siblings and I have good role models? Of course we do.

Let me relate one of the funny and smart things my parents would do. Friday night was their date night. They would always go out and have dinner and we would stay with a baby-sitter. Once in a while no babysitter would be available. Do you think my parents canceled their time together? No way. We would go to a restaurant and my father would ask for a table for four and a table for two at opposite ends of the restaurant. I loved the look of shock on the hostess' face. She would think my parents were kidding. They were not. We kids would eat by ourselves (and develop independence skills as well) and my parents would have 60 minutes for themselves – I call this not just parenting, but GENIUS.

Forget all the psychobabble, which suggests you are not doing enough for your kids. <u>My guess is that if you are buying this book you are a very conscientious parent who is likely doing too much for your kids and not enough for yourself</u>. Maybe it is time for you to do something for yourself. Maybe you should put this book down and go out for a nice dinner – without your kids!

REVIEW

Congratulations on making it through the most important chapter in the book. If you have decided not to read the chapter and just skip to the review, here are some things to keep in mind:

1. The most important thing you can do to be prepared for parenting is to make sure you are emotionally nourished and healthy. You must take care of your own emotional needs first. Tune into your needs, acknowledge your needs as a person, and provide yourself with the same positive nurturing you want to shower on your kids. If you take care of yourself first, you will be in the healthiest and most powerful position to help those you love most – your children.

2. If you are a two parent family then the foundation of that family is the relationship between Mother and Father. Therefore make sure you nurture and tend to that relationship as this behavior will trickle down to your kids and provide both comfort and a model for their lives and relationships. Other family configurations should focus on the adults having respectful, harmonious relationships with the other adults involved in the family, as again this provides a model your children will most likely adopt.

3. If you are burnt out and run down spend less time carting your kids to activities and more time on yourself and your needs. In this way you will be nourished and ready when your kids really need you.

Chapter 2

BE IN CONTROL OF YOUR OWN THOUGHTS AND MOOD

Too often I hear people express their emotions as if they just happen and there is nothing the person can do about them. Nothing could be further from the truth. Aside from people who have a biological mood disorder (and many of the techniques I have outlined work here as well), each of us has total responsibility for our own thoughts, moods, and therefore behaviors. The politically correct idea that we should all share our feelings, no matter what, is just harmful psychobabble. *What we should be doing is working on the way we think and feel so that we enter and engage in the world in the most meaningful and positive manner possible.* This is not just a skill. It is a responsibility. You control how you interpret the world and you control how you think about your life. Do it positively.

THE SUBCONSCIOUS

Consider the number of thoughts you can keep in consciousness at one point. It is a very small number. Yet we know a vast amount of information and use it constantly. But how do we do this if we are not actively processing this information? Well much of what we do everyday occurs at a subconscious level. Have you ever been driving your car and ended up at a location familiar to you but not your intended destination? While you were thinking of something else, your driving was on auto-pilot (controlled by your subconscious). You did not end up in some random place. You ended up at a place you knew, but just were not intending to drive. We are always giving ourselves messages that are affecting our behavior. Because of the limited space in our consciousness, we do this at the subconscious level. It is each of our responsibilities to get to know these hidden messages and create ones that are positive and supportive.

Let's look at an example I use when I am out public speaking. I ask all the members of the audience to stand (please do it as you are reading). Stretch both your arms out wide. Now drop your right arm to your right side and slide it down your leg getting as close to your ankle as you can. How close did you get? About 99% of my adult audiences get about halfway between their thigh and their ankle. Therefore about 99% are UNSUCCESSFUL in getting to their ankle. If I have a room full of kindergarteners and give them the exact same task they are about 100% successful. Why is that? Because they bend their knee and grab their ankle. Notice in my original directions I said nothing about bending (or not bending) your knee. The choice was yours. YOU decided NOT to bend your knee. You fed yourself a message that led to failure. The young kids did not feed themselves that message and therefore were free to succeed. You actually brought a barrier from your subconscious that resulted in failure. I bet that most of you did not even consciously think, "Hey, I better not bend my knee". You just reacted and did it. Why? Because you have been in this situation about 100 times and you now react at a subconscious level to it. You fed yourself information, not consciously, which created the difference between success and failure.

Now the task I gave you is something you rarely do. Just imagine the number of messages you give to yourself, about yourself, everyday that are subconscious and ingrained. This is why we often talk in therapy about making the subconscious- conscious. If you can actually inspect the messages you are feeding yourself you have a much better chance at shaping those messages yourself.

Another verification of the importance of the subconscious can be seen in the fact that we have marketing companies. Marketers know that most decisions are not based on the product but on the associations you have to that product. And how do you form associations to products? Well the marketing companies try to insert them into your conscious and subconscious.

I remember a car advertisement that was very succinct; 'Buying a Mercedes – Genius'. If you see this enough you may start equating this car with your intellect (I knew this was false since at the time I owned a Mustang which was really genius). I saw a liquor advertisement the other day that said that this liquor was only 'Fit for a King'. Don't you like to think of yourself as a King? The fact is, most people are quite easily manipulated if you feed them statements that they incorporate into their subconscious.

So part of your job as a parent is to make sure that your messages are positive and that your outlook is optimistic. You do this by constantly reviewing your subconscious messages and replacing the negative ones with ones which are realistic and true. Therefore, if you make a parenting mistake, you are not a 'bad parent'; you are 'someone who has made an error at this moment'. If your spouse did something foolish, they are not an 'inconsiderate spouse', they are 'someone who made a mistake that is rectifiable'. Just by taking the time to inspect the way you assess your behavior and others behavior, gives you the opportunity to change the way you think, and therefore feel, about it.

ALL OR NONE STATEMENTS

Often people have all or none statements in their head. "If my friend does not call me today they do not like me anymore". "If I do not get everything done on my list today I am a failure". You can probably think of 50 of these. These thoughts are caustic and are the seeds of depression and anxiety. Your friend may love you but have a crisis today or just be too busy. Your list may be too long or you may run into unforeseen delays. Allowing messages like these to play on you only opens the door for negative thinking and depression.

I could write an entire book on the messages that people give themselves which lead to their being depressed or angry or frustrated or happy or content, etc. (maybe I will do it next). However, this is a book about parenting. So let's cut to the chase and state it. It is your job as a parent to prune your negative subconscious thoughts. Only in this way will you be able to help your children learn to control their thoughts and moods. After all, they will either control their own thoughts or thoughts will be fed to them through cable TV, marketing firms, the Internet etc.

HAPPINESS/POSITIVISM

Given what I have just written you can see that I believe it is a moral obligation for people to be positive. The idea that we should just act on our feelings all the time is a primitive one. After all, if you are angry when your child comes home do you think it is appropriate that you take it out on him? Of course not. You have an obligation to put forth your best effort to ensure that he is taken care of and happy. You can certainly acknowledge feelings like depression, etc., but they should not be acted upon as if you have a right to disseminate this negativity to all in your environment. Your job as a parent and teacher is to help your child acknowledge his feelings while helping him to modulate them to act in a positive manner.

It is up to each one of us how we are going to view the world and what face we are going to share with others – especially our loved ones. There is a tremendous talk show host/author/teacher by the name of Dennis Prager who speaks often about the morality of happiness. I invite you to look up his website at www.Dennisprager.com.

The point is that you have a choice on how you view the world. This is one of the things your children will notice most about you and one of the things that you will instill most in your children.

By way of example, Pamela, a 37 year-old woman came to see me complaining about her husband of 15 years. She stated he did not love her and avoided her. I decided to meet with him individually to get his side of the story. He assured me he loved and admired his wife. However, for the past 8 years he had been avoiding her because it was too painful for him to be constantly criticized and rejected by someone he loved. When we all met together I asked the husband to start the session. He once again pledged his love and admiration for his wife. He literally laid his heart on the table as she sat silently listening. I then turned to her for a reaction. She said, "What did I tell you, the guy does not love me". When I suggested that she must have misheard because it was painfully obvious how much he loved her, she said "Yeah, I heard him, *but he doesn't mean it*". I can assure you if you interpret everything negatively, and twist messages so they are malignant, you will have a dreary and painful life.

I will end this section by describing a beautiful picture I have in my office. It is of a rose growing out of a rose bush. Below it is the following caption:

> *I can complain because rosebushes have thorns,*
> *or rejoice because the thorn bush has a rose……*
> IT IS ALL UP TO ME.

PERSPECTIVE

When you are in control of your thoughts and fears you tend to be able to put things in much better perspective. I received a lovely Christmas card from a young high school student I treated in middle school. At one point in her life she had only received A's. The pressure on her to never get a B was self-inflicted and stifling. She was actually afraid to go to school for fear she might get a B. When we spoke we discussed how this was self-inflicted, and she could change it. We actually made an agreement that we would do the 'B cheer' when she got one.

In her card to me she wrote she had received her first D this semester and it did not end her world (she noted she did some extra credit and brought it up to a C). The point she made was that she had been afraid of something due to her own thoughts. When she challenged them she saw she was still extremely smart and that the

D-C changed nothing. She was still smart, and would always be, regardless of this one grade.

I had a college student who came to me. He was afraid he was going to fail one of his classes and have to retake it in summer school in order to graduate. He was in a complete panic stating "This would ruin my life". I suggested he come in and help me with one of my other clients. He seemed a little shocked but asked for more information. I told him she was a young mother who had just been diagnosed with breast cancer. I said "What a relief it will be for her to hear about someone who has a much worse problem than hers. The possibility that you may have to take a 6 week accounting course in the summer surely is a much greater problem than her cancer. I can't wait to have you talk to her". He got the sarcasm as well as the point (and as an aside he graduated on time).

Parents sometimes fall into this trap as well. They will encounter an issue with their adolescent and engage in a two-step process: Panic and then Think. I try to encourage parents to skip the first step (since it usually leads to hysteria) and focus on the second step. I had a mom call me regarding her high school senior named Jeff. Jeff was a very nice kid, who got into a little trouble here and there, but never anything serious. The mom was very loving (which can lead to some over protectiveness). She stated she thought her son was 'huffing', a process where kids inhale vapors from various sources which can get them high. This was way out in left field so I asked why she thought Jeff was a 'huffer'. "Well" she said, "I found a can of shaving cream that was mangled in the trash". I asked if she jumped from this directly to concluding her son was a serious drug addict who needed immediate hospitalization. She said, "What else can I conclude"? I suggested that before we hospitalize Jeff she ask him about it. When he came home from school (where this 'huffer' spent the day), she asked him and he confirmed that it was part of a science project he had done. He had made an error with that can but had been successful on his next attempt and had received an A on the project. Now, whenever his mom gets on him about anything, he lets her know that is what 'huffers' do. He is still a pretty funny guy.

In a similar vein, I had a very funny mom come to my office. She had a 10 year-old daughter named Sarah who was plucking her eyelashes out. Sarah was experiencing some anxiety and this was the manner in which she expressed it. The mom was absolutely crushed. There was a lot of crying going on. When I inquired why she felt this was such a big problem, she said, "For goodness sake, if this does not stop she will be attending her prom with no eyelashes and be the laughing stock of the dance". I actually laughed and asked why she was not focusing even farther down the line, like at Sarah's wedding.

Sarah was a cute, fun-loving, 5th grader. I assured the mom that we would work on it here. I also told her a very positive experience was around the corner. Her child was at the age where peer pressure was about to take hold. Although peer pressure gets a bad rap, it does a wonderful job of smoothing out the edges of young people. It's one thing for your mom to say, "Don't pull out your eyelashes". It is quite another for some kids at school to say, "You look funny". Under this kind of pressure kids usually give up their quirks. We worked together for a year and resolved the issue. Upon our last session I asked Sarah why she thought she had changed. She said "I don't want to look funny at school". Throughout the year the mom had kept very low key and allowed Sarah to grow. I respected that she kept her own 'mom anxiety' under control and allowed her daughter to beat this issue without catastrophizing. Well done Mom and well done Sarah. By the way I fully expect to get a 2018 prom picture with Sarah, eyelashes and all.

It is your job as a parent to help your child to understand the difference between a crisis and a problem that has solutions. Think and ask before you jump to conclusions. Too many times perspective and priority are lost as each step on the ladder is fraught with 'perceived' disaster, which is not really there.

Years ago in one of my psychology books I saw a meaningful picture that I wish I had kept. It was a split frame picture, meaning it had two pictures juxtaposed in the same frame, one on the left side and one on the right. On the left was a picture of a bright sunny day with 3, 4 and 5 year olds playing in a park. You could see the elation and wonder on their faces as they played. Joy was everywhere. Next to it was a picture of a dark and dreary day in NY City with adults trudging out of a subway while it was drizzling. All of them had solemn down-trodden faces as they shuffled to their next challenge. They appeared truly depressed. Underneath the picture was a two-word caption: "What Happened?"

The point is it is up to us to be happy. As children, most of us felt that way, but along the way life tends to get us down. Be more like a kid today – Enjoy.

REVIEW

1. How we think can change the way we feel.

2. Thinking is not a passive act; it is something we can control. How we interpret events will shape how we feel about those events.

3. The subconscious is a very powerful reservoir of thoughts we have had so many times that they have become part of who we are. Some of these are not useful and actually make life harder. It is up to each parent to assess their subconscious thoughts so they can throw out those thoughts that make life more difficult. They will then be in a better place to help their children do this.

4. 'All or None' thinking is a style which can cause people to misinterpret what has happened in their lives and over-react to minor misunderstandings or obstacles.

5. It is a moral obligation to be happy and spread positivism in your life. This is something you can control and should be a foundation of your parenting.

6. It is the job of every parent to provide perspective for his or her children. Helping children and adolescents to differentiate between problems and crises is part of a parent's responsibility.

CHAPTER 3

THE FIVE MYTHS OF PSYCHOTHERAPY

If after reading this book, you decide you or your child/adolescent or your family should try out therapy, I want you to have a good idea of what to look for and what to expect in therapy. The average person knows so little about psychotherapy and most of what they do know is misinformation fed to them by television shows or movies. Thus, this is an attempt to teach people what psychotherapy is really all about.

I was speaking to a group of concerned parents regarding their children. A topic I frequently discuss is self-esteem and ways parents can enhance this in themselves and their children. After the presentation, when most people had left, one woman came up to me and asked me the question "What is psychotherapy anyway?" At first the importance of this inquiry escaped me, but as we spoke I was once again confronted with the lesson that people in our society know very little about the practice of psychology and how it can be helpful.

Let me explain psychotherapy by dispelling some myths which have been created by watching such shows as 'One Flew over the Cuckoo's Nest', 'Sybil' and so forth.

MYTH 1: PEOPLE WHO ENTER PSYCHOTHERAPY ARE CRAZY.

In fact, they are more stable than most. I make it a point to share with my patients that I never really get to work with people who have the biggest problems because they are the ones who lack the courage and insight to face a problem and remedy it. On the contrary, every person I see has already shown they have both the insight to realize that something is going wrong and the courage to say "I want to change this".

MYTH 2: THERAPY IS VERY PAINFUL.

Therapy does not have to be painful unless you feel that learning about yourself, and living a more fulfilling life, is painful. Learning about one's self can be very gratifying, uplifting, and enjoyable. This goes double for families who learn not only about themselves but about each other as well. I know that when I learn the lessons that stick most are the ones I had fun learning. Play therapy works well with children, but having fun and learning are inextricably tied together at every stage of life. Granted, there are times when dealing with traumatic, emotional issues can be painful, but understanding them, and coming to grips with them can be extremely exciting. Families who go through this process often feel the exhilaration of truly enjoying each other and developing closer and stronger ties with one another.

MYTH 3: THE THERAPIST TELLS YOU WHAT TO DO AND THINGS GET BETTER

Who knows you better than you? No one, including your therapist. The hallmark of positive psychotherapy is not working "on" people but working "with" them. Therapists learn to work with their patients. The patient, after all, is the one who will know if things are getting better in his or her life. In this way therapy is like a smorgasbord. Sure, the therapist cooks many of the plates, but the patient only samples them before choosing which ones he or she wants. Hopefully, whatever he or she chooses will help the situation. If it does not, feel free to sample some other ideas.

MYTH 4: IF I GO TO A PSYCHOLOGIST, IT MEANS I CAN'T SOLVE MY OWN PROBLEMS.

Two points are important here. First, every person is faced with some difficulties which seem insurmountable. To be able to see that one needs help at these times is a sign of emotional strength not weakness (we all know someone who has been dealing with the same problem for years but does nothing about it – would you call that strength?). Second, psychologists do not sit and listen, then solve your problem and give you the answer. Psychologists help people develop coping strategies so you not only solve the present problem but can also deal with other problems in the future. If a problem were a boulder, it is your choice to lie under it and be crushed or climb to the top of it and reach new heights.

MYTH 5: YOU HAVE TO HAVE A MAJOR PROBLEM BEFORE CONSULTING A PSYCHOLOGIST.

One of the most interesting questions I ask people when they first come in to see me is how long they have been experiencing the present problem. Whether it is a family or an individual problem the answer usually ranges from 3-7 years. What this tells me is that most people are sensitive enough to pick up the cues of a problem in its infancy. However, we are trained to hope that they will remedy themselves. Waiting this long often results in a small problem becoming a bigger problem. The field of psychological problems is one where the adage 'An ounce of prevention is worth a pound of cure' is very true. If you feel something is not right, seek a consultation. If everything is fine, you will have peace of mind knowing it. If there is a problem, you will have the solace of knowing you can solve it much more easily now rather than five years from now.

These are just a few of the myths, which block people from obtaining therapy for themselves. My advice to people contemplating psychotherapy is – feel free to shop around and find a therapist with whom you and your family feel comfortable. You will be sharing some sensitive things with this person and you will want to feel a level of comfort and trust. You can then get started on changing things for the better.

REVIEW

This chapter highlights five of the most commonly held erroneous beliefs about psychotherapy.

1. People who enter psychotherapy are usually quite stable and determined. Most of them have the insight to realize they have an issue and the courage to deal with it.

2. Therapy can have difficult moments but is usually a positive experience as you learn about yourself.

3. Good therapists work "with" you, not "on" you. They are consultants with a specialty to help you see areas of your life and psyche, which may be hidden.

4. Psychologists are not going to "solve" your problems. You are going to solve them with the help of a psychologist who can guide you along the path to success; sharing insights and helping you develop coping techniques along the way.

5. Most people realize they have an issue when it is in its infancy. This is the time to treat it. Problems are much easier to treat in their infancy than when they have become a well-entrenched habit.

10 TRUTHS PARENTS SHOULD KNOW

CHAPTER 1

KIDS WANT GOOD LIVES

I have been practicing psychology for 25 years, and although I see many adult patients, I have a specialty in treating children, adolescents and families. One concept has always rung true to me: THE STUFF YOUR KID DOES IS MEANT TO MAKE HIS LIFE BETTER – really. I have never seen an adolescent who has said "You know what Doc, I want a crappy life and I think I can get there by doing X". Adolescents want what is good in their lives. However, they often err in knowing what to value. This is why I often refer to adolescents as Human Mistake Machines. For instance, imagine I tell you I have a mixture of various poisons I want you to ingest – you would call the police and have me arrested. However, many adolescents ingest meth in the mistaken belief that it will be fun, they will have a great experience, and they will have more friends.

Whenever I have an adolescent come up with a silly idea, or do a stupid thing, before helping, I always ask WHY? What was your motivation? What made this worth doing for you? I am amazed at the thinking that has gone into most ideas (after you get by the obligatory 'I don't know'). Yes, the logic is often convoluted, but it does make sense if you think about it as if you were 15.

By way of example of the outrageously foolish things that adolescents do, I had a mother bring her 17 year-old (Rich) to my office. She stated she wanted to show me a tape of Rich's accomplishments. Rich was surprised because he did not know his mom had kept such a tape but was happy to watch it with us. When we turned on the video there was Rich front and center. Interestingly, about 8 friends surrounded him at his house and they were all smoking dope. That's right, he had tape recorded he and his friends partying in his home. Not only that, during the taping, the phone rings (this is on the tape) and he picks it up. It is his mom and he gestures all to be quiet. He then proceeds to tell his mom he is studying with some friends and unfortunately will not be home when she gets home because he has more studying to do at another friend's house. He then hangs up and they all give him high fives and have a good laugh on what he just pulled off.

Needless to say Rich looked on in horror as we silently watched the tape. Where did the mom find this tape? Why she found it in her car where Rich inadvertently left it. He was bringing it to a friend's house to show the friend when he forgot it. Nice call Rich. I mean can you be more stupid than this? Without going into detail, Rich was almost grounded for life. The good news is that he graduated from an Ivy League school and has a very prestigious job lined up in New York City. However, at 17, few have been sillier.

Let's look at a few other examples from my practice, which highlight this concept.

I saw an adolescent named Colt, age 15. He was charged with vandalism for throwing eggs at the home of someone he knew. This is foolish and you know you are going to get caught. His rationale: the person had hurt one of his friends and he wanted him to know it was not OK. While wrong, I get it. He did not just get out of bed and say, "Hey I think I should egg a house". Now we have something deeper to talk about other than the foolishness of his behavior. We actually have a context in which to discuss his behavior and try to rectify it in the future.

As a parent of an adolescent you will be miles ahead if you understand his motivations. You have a much better platform from which to speak to him, and you will talk about issues which are much more relevant.

Let's take a look at Sean who was 16 when I met him.

Dr. Matt: Why were you smoking dope at school?

Sean: I wanted this guy to be my friend.

Issue: We need to talk about how to make friends and how to choose more reasonable people for friendship.

How about Bill who had just turned 17 when he came to see me?

Dr. Matt: Why did you divulge your friend's complaints to his teacher?

Joanne: I thought his points were right and the teacher would see it that way.

Issue: We need to discuss boundaries and how to help a friend stand up for himself – if he wants to.

It's easy to see why the life of an adolescent often seems like a ship on rough waters – being tossed about because of their decisions. DO NOT GET IN THE BOAT WITH YOUR ADOLESCENT. Rather make sure you are like Poseidon (God of the Sea) understanding the ocean and helping to re-route the boat where necessary. The goal is usually good; it's the route to it that often needs to change.

Let me end this chapter by noting that I have a framed picture hanging above one of the doors in my office. It is from the book Children's Letters to God. It says simply: 'Dear God, I am doing the best I can. (signed) Frank'. I ask people to remember this about their children. They should remember it about themselves as well (almost all parents are doing the best they can).

REVIEW

1. I have never met an adolescent who wants a bad life. All the things they do are geared toward making their lives better. It is up to you as a parent to uncover their motivation. Only then will you have the possibility of creating real change.

2. Remember that your adolescent (and you) is doing the best he can. I know that is sometimes hard to believe but it is true.

3. As a parent, if you understand your adolescent's motivation you have a much better chance at helping him to develop positive plans to achieve his goals.

4. Understanding the context in which your adolescent made a decision allows you an avenue to explore the decision in greater detail and come up with alternative (and better) ways to deal with an issue.

CHAPTER 2

HOW DID MY KID KNOW THAT?

(QUALITATIVE/DEVELOPMENTAL LEAPS)

There are times when I will get a call from a parent who has a child who has undergone a childhood trauma. The call will go something like this.

Parent: Hello Dr. Matt

Dr. Matt: Hello

Parent: I have a strange thing going on. I have a 13 year-old son whose dad passed away when he was 8. All of a sudden he is full of questions about this and seems to be showing a lot of fear about my dying. It is like he is reliving the experience all over again.

My response to this is that he IS reliving it and it is a GOOD sign. What this tells you is that your child has reached a new cognitive/emotional level in his life. I do not mean he has just grown older; he has qualitatively changed the way he sees and processes his life and the world around him. What is happening is like an entire change in a computer's operating system. All of a sudden he takes this new, more sophisticated program and tries to understand his life up until now. Most things are easily incorporated, but traumatic events and situations that have no real answer must now be 'downloaded ' using the new software and that takes some work.

For instance, an explanation of death, and what happened at age 8, no longer suffices for a more insightful and understanding 13 year-old. He needs a more sophisticated explanation to understand this trauma as well as his feelings around it.

In fact, I tell parents who have a child who has undergone this kind of event that there will probably be two or three qualitative changes in perception and understanding over time and each time it will be like experiencing the death anew (sad in some ways but encouraging in others). This it is not a time to get upset but rather a time to help the child understand what happened, talking to their new level of understanding and awareness. It is also not a time to think, "I should have done a better job explaining this years ago". I am sure you did a great job, it is just your child has a whole new level of awareness and must be given a new set of explanations that fit his new developmental level.

While the death of a parent is an extreme example, I see this in a much more subtle way in both therapy and at home with my own kids. This is where parents get a little frustrated and I will admit I used to when I was a less experienced therapist.

For instance, I will be working on an issue with an adolescent. We are not getting anywhere but I continue to discuss my points and the adolescent continues to discuss his or hers. Then one day the adolescent will enter therapy and tell me I am a bit confused, but he has figured out how to handle his issue on his own. He will then regurgitate (sometimes verbatim) exactly what I have been saying the last 6 months. He will assure me he wished I could have helped but he heard this on television or at a friend's house or just thought it up. There is generally no appreciation that we have covered this ground before and I can see why parents would get frustrated and want to say, "I have been telling you this all along"!

At these times please remember (and remind yourself) this is a good sign. This means your adolescent is learning. Frankly, adolescents are much more likely to follow advice from themselves than from you. So if they think they thought of it themselves – applaud them. When this happens in therapy I actually ask them if I can write down what they said because it is so insightful and I may want to use it in other sessions. This allows the adolescent to see that I am very positive about this change and that it has great value.

When adolescents get better in this way it also allows me to know that the child is growing and that their prognosis has just gotten much better. Does it really matter who said it - YES - it is actually more important that the adolescent ascribes the thought and behavior change to himself rather than you. Parents need to support this even though you may have said it until you were blue in the face.

My favorite example of this was when I met a 17 year-old named Dan who was making a decision about moving to a high school in a different state. He was going to live with his girlfriend's family (who he did not know very well) and his parents were surprisingly receptive to this move. I suggested to the parents that this plan was fraught with problems and would probably end in heartbreak and loneliness. They told me their philosophy was that it was Dan's decision. After much discussion with Dan he proudly came in to me one day and we had the following conversation.

Dan: Dr. Matt, I am not sure you are helping me.

Dr. Matt: Really? What's up?

Dan: This idea about moving is not a good one. My girlfriend and I might break up and living in a different state with no one I know except her would be pretty tough. Also everyone knows me in my current school and I would really miss all my friends.

Dr. Matt: That's a very interesting insight. I am curious where you came up with it (knowing full well we had covered this ground approximately 1 million times).

Dan: I was listening to music last night and it suddenly occurred to me. I mean it just came to me so I started to think about it and then I spoke to my friends about it and they agreed.

Dr. Matt: Well I am extremely impressed with how well thought out your ideas are on this subject and I am sorry we did not discuss it at the level to which you have taken it. Do you mind if I write it down because it is really a lot for me to digest all at once and I might want to review it later.

Dan: Yeah, that's cool.

Prologue: Dan did not move and ended up having a stellar senior year in high school. He lettered on his sport's team and was on the honor roll. He was accepted to the college of his choice and his girlfriend and he decided to remain friends as they went to different colleges.

REVIEW

1. Your child will learn about the world throughout his life. However, there will be times when he has a qualitative change in his understanding of the world. It will seem like he has changed overnight. These moments will happen a number of times during a child's development. What is difficult, at these times, is to take traumatic and challenging issues that were understood at a younger developmental level, and explain them in a way that works with the child's new understanding. It is up to you as a parent to explain these things in the language of the new understanding.

2. This occurs in more subtle ways when kids and adolescents suddenly explain to you something you have been saying for quite a while but they have ignored. Suddenly they are 'explaining' it to you like you never said a word. Remember this is good for two reasons. The first is that they are reaching new heights in their understanding. The second is that if they believe they thought of this on their own they are much more likely to follow it. Your job is to go outside for a quick run to avoid screaming at them "I said that a million times already!" Good luck.

CHAPTER 3

THE MANY FACES OF MATURITY

This is one of those beliefs which constantly astounds me. I will hear from parents that their child is very mature. When I ask them 'in what' they seem confused. The idea for most parents is that your child is either mature or immature. This is a simplistic belief. Kids mature at DIFFERENT RATES IN DIFFERENT AREAS (i.e., physically, emotionally, athletically, intellectually, socially, etc.) and it is vitally important for parents not to mix these areas up and assume because a child is mature in one area he is mature in others.

Let me give you an example, which occurs in my office once or twice a year. I will have an adolescent, who is experiencing some social issues in school, come to see me. Many times these kids are extremely bright and could test out of high school. The inevitable parent question is should I send my 16 year-old to college now so they can 'fit in better' and have a new start. In my 25 years I have recommended this only one time (and for a very specific reason). All the other times I have counseled parents away from this misstep. I cannot tell you the number of young adults I have run into who now (in their twenties) thank me for this piece of guidance.

Why not move them up if they are having social problems? For precisely that reason. They are INTELLECTUALLY mature but SOCIALLY immature. The fact that they can solve a quadratic equation is not a good reason to send them to college where they will be faced with even tougher social situations. They need to grow up a little while longer and get help with the social side of things (and as you will learn this is a better predictor of their future success than grades). Your child, if he is smart, will always be smart. But if he is struggling socially he needs to learn social skills, and learn to apply them with same aged peers.

Let's take another example that is quite prominent these days. I will see a child in my practice, who is ATHLETICALLY mature.

He will decide that he is in high school to hone his athletic talents at the expense of his grades. By the time he is a twelfth grader he is more mature in athletics than most of us will ever be, but intellectually he is not mature. I am shocked how most parents will just overlook this immaturity because the child is a good athlete. Very few adolescents become pro athletes and even fewer make enough money in this short window to live comfortably the rest of their lives. Substituting current athletic prowess for lifetime success via education is a costly parenting error. Again, maturity in one area does not necessarily mean maturity in others.

    A story highlighting this concept could be seen in one of the best high school athletes I have ever met. He was an 18 year-old volleyball player named Stan. He was extremely accomplished and had Olympic aspirations, with good reason. However Stan decided that school was just not important. He was attending a college prep school and the academic work was challenging. His parents ran a lot of interference for him and got him through high school, even though Stan did not really deserve to graduate. As they would say to me "He is a gifted athlete, the rest is just stuff he does". It is dangerous to put this much emphasis on one area of an adolescent's life to the exclusion of the rest. Stan left to play volleyball in Europe. The last time I saw him I was out with my wife. I wish I could say it was a fun experience. We were at a restaurant where a young man opened the door for us. It was Stan. I was happy to see him. I asked him how old he was and he replied 26. I asked if he was still playing volleyball and he said he had torn his MCL in Europe and was never the same. I then asked what he was doing now. He said he was the door person right here....at this restaurant. UGGGGHHHHH!

    EMOTIONAL maturity should not be overlooked as well. I was listening to a talk show on the radio one day as I was driving. In a Midwestern city a 13 year-old boy had become upset in school. After school he ran home, grabbed his dad's gun and went back and shot another boy. Fortunately, the other boy lived and the show was dedicated to how we need to teach our kids how to use guns to minimize this kind of thing happening again. On the show was a guest advocating that all children be taken out and taught HOW to use a gun and about gun safety. There were many calls to the show either for or against this idea. I pulled over and called in because they were all missing the point. The father had trained his son in gun safety and gun usage. The training appeared to be quite thorough and his 13 year-old really understood guns. In fact, had he had taken a test regarding gun ownership and safety, I am sure he would have passed at the 90% level. What the parent did not seem to understand is that the boy understood INTELLECTUALLY how to use a gun, he understood PHYSICALLY how to use guns, but he had not developed the EMOTIONAL MATURITY to control his own emotions. Thus his emotional immaturity is what led to this problem, not a lack of understanding regarding guns. There-in was the problem. More information would have done nothing – he already knew it all. However, he was 13 years old emotionally and he had been ridiculed at school. He FELT he needed to do something. If he were given a quiz with a question which stated 'Should you shoot someone if you get mad at them'; he would have answered 'No'. The point is that he was not emotionally mature enough to be allowed access to guns and so this happened.

REVIEW

1. People look at maturity as a unitary concept. Don't be fooled - it is not. When you are raising a child or adolescent you want them to mature in all areas – physically, emotionally, intellectually, etc.

2. Kids and adolescents mature in different areas of their lives at vastly different times. For instance, different adolescents mature physically at different ages. In addition, no adolescent I know matures in all areas at the same time. Some areas of growth appear quickly and some areas lag behind.

3. As parents it is important for you to keep an eye on all the balls in the air, not just the brightly colored one or two. Putting too much emphasis in one area at the expense of others is very risky.

4. Regardless in which areas adolescents first mature, someday your child will most likely have to count on their well roundedness to get them by in life.

CHAPTER 4

THE HOLY GRAIL OF ADOLESCENCE –

THE PLEASURE AND PAIN PRINCIPLE

Do you know what principle adolescents use to make decisions in their lives? They use the pleasure/pain principle. You simply engage in those behaviors, which result in pleasure and avoid those, which result in pain. Just think about it. Kids love video games. Why? One of the reasons is that video games are so easy to figure out. The rules are basic and clear and do not change depending on your child's behavior, mood, etc. Good decisions lead to pleasure, bad ones lead to pain.

THE NOW VS THE FUTURE

A crucial caveat to keep in mind in regards to the pleasure/pain principle is that unlike most adults, adolescents respond to this principle within a very restricted time range. That is 'the future', for adolescents, usually consists of what is happening in the next 6 - 12 hours. For most adults the future is much longer than this. Therefore, when parents are considering how to negotiate with an adolescent, it is best to keep in mind that the sooner the reward or consequence the better. I will often hear parents bemoan the fact that their adolescent did not work hard for a great goal. When I ask about the contract, I hear that if the adolescent behaved well all semester, the family would go to Disney World in the summer. What would be much more effective is to allow computer time today for good behavior during school. I know of no adolescent who will forgo a fun event today because they will be fatigued tomorrow (I know many adults who will). Conversely, try to tell an adolescent that the benefit of working out in the gym is long-term health and you will get a blank stare. Tell him he will appear more attractive to the girl he likes and he will be at the gym.

My suggestion for parents is to start where the adolescent is in terms of their ability to understand time and rewards. Remember you, as parents, are much more capable of gauging your behavior over longer periods of time than is your adolescent.

THE PRINCIPLE IS CLEAR, CONSISTENT AND NON-EMOTIONAL

Have you ever seen your adolescent negotiating when his player got killed in a video game? No. Have you ever seen him write the manufacturer to get more goodies because the 'game is unfair'? Of course not. Why? Because the game will not respond – it will just keep doling out pleasure (success) or pain (failure) and adolescents understand and respect this concept. The reason he challenges you is that he is testing you. He wants to know where you will weaken and where he can shortcut the rules. This is not possible in the video world so there is no complaining, negotiating, or tantrum. There is only payoff or no payoff.

This is why kids are so good at figuring out ways around things. They are looking for pleasure – payoff now with the least amount of effort. It is your job as a parent to keep the scales balanced, even when your adolescent wants it to change.

Parents get upset when kids try to manipulate them to get their needs met. Be proud of this. It is a kid's job to try to get their 'pleasure' (meaning stuff they want) with the least 'pain' (in this case payment by work, etc.). It is a disabled kid who does not try to work around the rules a bit. Manipulation just means your kid has understood the rules and is trying to work around them. Appreciate it, but do not give into it.

My favorite story regarding the pleasure/pain principle (and its application) was with a 12 year-old girl named Christina who did not want to practice the piano. Her mom was furious as she was paying for the lessons. Christina, though, really did not want the 'pain' (practicing). However, upon examination the following behavioral pattern appeared. Christina did not want to go to lessons and each Monday the mom would ask her if she had practiced the piano. If she said "No", Mom would cancel the lesson (actually a pleasure for Christina). Guess what? She did not practice the next week with the same result. The mom thought canceling the lesson was 'pain' to Christina but all the while it was 'pleasure' and reinforcing her behavior.

What we decided to do was schedule a double lesson whenever Christina did not practice. This increased her 'pain' and got her to go back to practicing in order to reduce the lessons back to one hour.

REVIEW

1. Adolescents make almost all their decisions by consulting the 'pleasure/pain' principle. If it is pleasurable they do it. If it is painful they avoid it.

2. The 'future' for most adolescents consists of about one day. Therefore, using short-term goals and rewards will result in your adolescent working harder for the 'pleasure'.

3. It is your adolescent's job to try to manipulate you (get the pleasure without the pain). It is your job to respond in a straightforward, non-emotional manner to these attempts.

CHAPTER 5

HOW YOU SAY IT OFTEN MATTERS MORE THAN WHAT YOU SAY

By style I mean HOW you say something. By substance I mean WHAT you are saying. This may not seem logical, but it is almost always true. This does not mean that you should have nothing to say. You should have a point to make, but understand that after a relatively short period of time, how you say something is often more important to the listener than what you say in terms of being heard and considered.

All you have to do is take a look at your own life. When people approach you in a positive, respectful manner, you tend to listen to them, even if they are not saying what you want to hear. People who approach you in a bombastic, confronting, disrespectful manner, are almost always ignored – even if you agree with their viewpoint.

This is especially true in both marital therapy as well as work with adolescents. I often start off my presentations regarding working with adolescents with one big word - RESPECT. I know this is hard to do when your 16 year-old just lied to you, snuck out, and got into a car accident. But after you take a few breaths, and decide to speak with him, do it with respect and you are far more likely to be heard.

I believe that if you look at your own experiences you will see the wisdom of this advice. However, let me offer up two research threads which also bolster this idea.

The first thread has to do with what people actually remember and take away from a presentation. If the material is kept the same but the lecturers' styles are varied, an interesting phenomenon occurs. When people are asked, a few days later, to give their impression of the lecture (positive/negative) most people list things they heard the lecturer say to support their opinions. If this is done again about 6 weeks later, something different occurs.

Now, very few of the respondents will remember a lot of the specific points made. What now shapes their impressions was the style of the presenter. Was he positive? Did he seem involved in the presentation? Did he come across as excited? Was he enthusiastic? This is how people record the lecture in their long-term memory and it shapes whether they 'liked' it or not. Thus you can see that how you say something has a very important effect on the listener, sometimes more important than the content.

Another good example comes from a book written by John Gottman, PH.D. (Why Marriages Succeed or Fail, 1994). Dr. Gottman studied couples to ascertain if he could isolate factors which would accurately predict which engaged couples would be successful in marriage and which would not. When the factors were isolated, he found his predictive ability to be over 80% (and 96% for predicting which couples would stay together at least three years). How did he do this? He examined HOW people fought. Couples, whose fights included respect for the other and an appreciation for the other's point of view, even when disagreeing, were far more compatible than those who did not. People who would soon be divorced tended to fight by insulting one another's character and being disrespectful to the person rather than focusing on the argument. The issues being argued made no difference at all. Again, if you want to be heard and keep a good relationship start by using respect as a bonding tool and go from there.

Most people hear about these studies, reflect on their own lives, and say of course – that is obvious. However, putting it into action is sometimes difficult. Remember to approach the adolescent the way you would like to be approached. You can always go with a heavy-handed approach, so why not start with something more respectful.

Let's do a little thought experiment. Think back to your favorite teacher in school. Think about why that teacher was your favorite and what you would say to him if he were here today. When I ask this I never hear anyone say, "because of the material he taught me". Most of you, when you are thinking, are thinking about a teacher who cared about you, someone you trusted, someone who believed in you, respected you, and appreciated you as a person. You probably don't remember the specific material they taught you. You remember how he approached you and the way he felt about you. My guess is you tried harder in these classes and actually learned more, but that is not what you carry with you as you go through life is it?

One of my favorite teachers was Mr. Willy. He was our 5th grade teacher. That's the year I learned that fun and learning not only go hand in hand, they feed off one another (I had other fun teachers but this was the year I really began to appreciate the HOW of teaching). Mr. Willy would pull down all the large shades in the classroom – our windows were about 7 feet high. He would then walk around the classroom, Socratic-style, and call on people, asking questions about the material. If you got it right, he would give you one of the tennis balls he was carrying and let you heave it into the shade which would make it shoot up with a very cool noise while he shouted "CORRECT". We loved it and instead of being afraid of being called upon, every hand was up for every question. He knew how to pull kids in and make it fun and he always did it in a positive manner.

When I received my Ph.D., I wrote to Mr. Willy to thank him for helping reinforce in me a love of learning and for showing me how fun it could be. Can I tell you exactly what I learned? No (otherwise I would be on that show 'Are You Smarter Than a 5th Grader'), but I can tell you I use his style in my therapy all the time. I knew he cared about me and thought the world of me.

This kind of involvement was also apparent when I took my internship at LAC/USC Medical Center. I was just out of graduate school. This would be my first 'real' job and I was expected to be a Ph.D. psychologist on staff.

My first supervisor was a man named Frank Acosta, Ph.D. Dr. Acosta was very well known and respected and deemed one of the better therapists around. He would be supervising/teaching me for most of the year. While I was happy with that, I knew I was in no way a seasoned therapist.

Dr. Acosta approached me the first day and asked me to record one of my sessions. I thought "Oh no, this is going to be a disaster". However, I complied and showed up to supervision, nervous, and with a tape in my hand.

The rest of our conversation went like this:

Dr. Acosta: Hello Matt. Welcome. What do you have there?

Intern Matt: I recorded my session this morning as you asked.

Dr. Acosta: Great, let's hear it.

The tape begins to roll and I begin to sweat profusely. After 10 minutes, which seem like three days, Dr. Acosta stops the tape.

Dr Acosta: Matt, I hear you laughing a lot with your patient on this tape.

Intern Matt: Yes

Dr. Acosta: I don't do enough of that in my sessions; perhaps you will be able to help me with that during our year together (reaches out to turn tape back on).

Intern Matt: (Head exploding, thinking): Did he just ask me to help him become a better therapist? Did he just say I do something he values? Did he just say he could learn from me? WHAT????????

Needless to say, after that moment no matter what he said to me (positive, negative or neutral) I willingly accepted. Why shouldn't I? The guy values me. I realized a long time later that he probably said this to put me at ease. I could have sneezed a lot on the tape and he would have said he needed to learn more about sneezing from me. The point was when he was in charge; he started off our relationship by noting something positive about me and allowing himself to be the student. This is one of the major reasons I always ask parents to have their child bring something in to my office they are proud of for our first session. I want to start by acknowledging their strengths and uniqueness and let them know I see all of them, especially the good stuff.

RESILIENCY THEORY

As researchers, it is always fascinating to see two specimens, placed in the same environment, turn out differently. This is especially true when the subjects being researched are human beings. Take two brothers, raised together, where one becomes very successful and the other flounders (there are numerous examples of this, but for arguments sake consider President Carter and his brother or President Clinton and his brother). This question has been thoroughly researched and has resulted in an explanation called resiliency theory. Somehow one of the brothers develop a kind of resilience and is able to fight through and become successful while the other brother is unable to do this. The question is how?

The answer seems to revolve around the successful individual having at least one adult who truly believed in his capabilities. A mentor, who cared about this individual, and allowed the individual to not only succeed but to believe he could keep succeeding in life. It is a little like infusing a human with the gift of confidence to get through the difficult times. This individual could be a parent but does not need to be. It does have to be someone stable in the child's life, who reinforced in the child that they are someone important.

When these dyads are interviewed this one factor seems to trump all the others. One of the people had a benevolent mentor, and someone who really believed in him. That alone can be the difference between success and lack of success.

I remember a particularly poignant example from my own life. I was at a professional hockey game with my mother. The Buffalo Sabres were playing and I was 12 years old. I had played hockey since I was 5 and I turned to my mom and said, "Someday I am going to be a pro hockey player". I was just joking around with her and thought she would banter something funny back about losing my teeth or some other reason not to follow this path. At first she did not respond at all so I said it again. She then turned toward me and said "Matthew, I have no doubt that if you set your mind to becoming a pro hockey player, you will. I believe you have the ability to do anything you set your mind to". I was not expecting this. I was stunned into silence. Is it shocking I can recall this moment as if it happened yesterday? I don't think so. Having someone believe in you at this level is a gift that will never be forgotten.

I will end this chapter by sharing one of my favorite poems. I think it speaks to the importance of maintaining a focus on what is important rather than being carried away by inconsequential minutia.

I Taught Them All
By Naomi White

I have taught in high school for ten years. During that time I have given assignments, among others, to a murderer, a pugilist, a thief and an imbecile. The murderer was a quiet little boy who sat on the front seat and regarded me with pale blue eyes: the pugilist lounged by the window and let loose at intervals with a raucous laugh that startled even the geraniums: the thief was a gay-hearted Lothario with a song on his lips: and the imbecile, a shifty-eyed little animal seeking the shadows.

The murderer awaits death in the state penitentiary; the pugilist lost an eye in a brawl in Hong Kong; the thief, by standing on tiptoe, can see the window of my room from the county jail; and the once gentle-eyed little moron beats his head against a padded wall in the state asylum.

All these pupils once sat in my room, sat and looked at me gravely across worn brown desks. I must have been a great help to these pupils....I taught them the rhyming scheme of the Elizabethan sonnet and how to diagram a complex sentence.

Sometimes it is important to get away from the task at hand and focus on the individual person in front of you. By supporting and encouraging him as an individual, you have a far greater chance of altering his life's course for the better. Stuff will come and go; valuing individuals at a deep level is what changes people for the better.

REVIEW

1. Most parents fret over WHAT they are going to say to their adolescent. Just as important is HOW you say something. Like most of us, when we are approached in a calm and respectful manner we tend to evaluate what is said to us in a more serious and thoughtful manner. Conversely, when we are approached in an accusatory, negative manner we tend to react by disregarding and ignoring what is said to us.

2. Not surprisingly, what we remember most about others in our lives tends to revolve around HOW they treat us not what they say.

3. When parenting it is important to remember these lessons so that you can approach your adolescent in a manner which will allow your point to be heard.

4. All people get in arguments from time to time. If you want your relationship to endure and even grow from these moments, then disagree with respect. People, who argue about points while always respecting the other person, tend to have relationships that grow from these moments. People, who attack each other personally, tend to have relationships that wither and die.

5. Research has shown that having just one person in a child's life, who truly believes in that child and communicates this regularly to the child in terms of words and actions, can be enough to help that child become successful.

CHAPTER 6

FRAMES ARE EVERYTHING

People frequently want to know how to change the opinions of kids. It's simple – use frames that work for kids. What is a frame you ask? Well, that is simple. It is the CONTEXT in which you place a behavior, thought, statement, etc. It is the part of the sentence or statement, which classifies it.

Let's take a look at a research study I ran and review how the cigarette companies FRAME their product.

Why would anyone smoke? I mean think about it. If I said to you I have developed a product, which will inevitably kill you, but on the way it will systematically destroy your body. Would you go out and buy it? I hope not (If you would, please put this book down and head to the nearest psychiatric facility). So, how do tobacco companies get kids to smoke? They FRAME the product into being 'cool and cuddly'. Look at their advertising. It is geared toward kids because the companies know, if kids do not start young, they will not start at all. It is a rare adult who says 'I have decided to take up smoking'. So let's look at how they do it and in what frames they put cigarettes.

Who does not want to be the Marlboro Man (a rebel out on his own, dashing, girls love him, boys want to be him)? Oh yeah, he is smoking a death stick too. In fact the death stick is front and center and part of 'The Man'. Look at how Cool Joe Camel is with his sunglasses. He's the life of the party, the guy everyone wants to hang with. What's right in front of him? Why his cigarette – of course he is cool. This is what we mean by frames, and the tobacco companies really have it down.

With all this pressure, why would kids STOP smoking. Well, I ran that very research project in Amherst, NY and presented the results at the Eastern Psychological Conference in the late 1980's. Now, of course, we have combated these frames with information on the dangers of smoking. Of course every kid in America knows that smoking is harmful. In fact, in my research, 99% of kids knew smoking was harmful and could give at least one accurate example of that harm. 99%!!! Education is working - the kids know the data. But guess what? It has limited to no effect on smoking patterns for kids. When kids are asked why they quit smoking their answers were "It looked stupid", "People will think I am an idiot", "Losers smoke", etc. These are all social frameworks. Not one of the top 5 reasons had anything to do with health effects.

This is one of the most powerful examples of frames at work. Kids are making their decisions based on what they consider cool and what their peer group considers cool, not health effects. Therefore, if you want your kid not to smoke, point at smokers and give them a label. For instance, "Look at that guy smoking – he must be a loser". "Wow that girl with the cigarette is kind of cute but that cigarette makes her look ugly". This is what prevents kids from getting into smoking. Your lungs will turn black – NOT a factor.

Frames are one of the most powerful tools parents have in dealing with adolescents. When adolescents see their behavior framed in a negative light they are much less likely to engage in that behavior. After all, most of the time they are doing it, it is because they are telling themselves it is cool. Your job is to change the frame in a matter-of-fact, almost invisible, manner.

Let me give you another example of a young woman in my practice who used to cut herself. The wounds were not very deep but they were plentiful. As always with 'cutters', the possibility of doing some severe damage, including killing herself accidentally, existed.

Carrie (age 16) would joyously show her family and friends her newest cuts. This was done for pure shock value, but as most of you are aware, if you do it enough you may make a mistake and hurt yourself.

During my second session with Carrie I asked her about the cutting. She told me her friends couldn't believe it. They were always checking it out and seeing if she was still doing it. The secondary gain she was getting (all this attention) was well worth the scars to her. In fact, it became clear that the frame she was using to reinforce her cutting was that she was seen as cool and people wanted to check in with her all the time. And it was not just female friends. Boys seemed fascinated with the cutting and she was getting a lot of attention.

I told her I wanted to see. She rolled up her sleeve and showed me. I thanked her and also let her know how proud I was that it was under her sleeve. When she asked why, I suggested that the cuts should be hidden. She was surprised by my answer. I said, in a calm and assuring tone, "The cutting suggests you are a self destructive person and the only way you can get attention is to hurt yourself. You are smart to keep these hidden as others will see you as someone not to hang with, but rather to ridicule and view as a side show freak". She was confused. I was giving her a compliment (she is smart), but adding a frame that people do not admire cutters. They are frightened by them and often do not associate with them. I told her that others are not paying attention because they think it is cool; rather there is always one stooge in a group who is stupid enough to do the really foolish things. The others usually set this stooge up and get her to keep doing it. I told her I found it hard to believe she did not realize this because each time she did this she was cementing her status. She began to see that this was the reason she did not get asked to go to parties (even though these same girls crowded around her to look at her cuts while at school). This was also the reason she was not asked out despite the attention boys gave her during school hours. I could have spent our time talking to her about the dangers of cutting, or looked deeply into her emotional pain, but that would have missed the point that what was motivating her was her frame that this was cool.

Destroying the framework eliminated the behavior. Now she openly states that cutting is uncool, and she will not return to that level of 'uncoolness'. This new framework will assure it. (Again a caveat. If she had been cutting due to strong psychological pain inside of her – which is sometimes the case - this intervention would not have been used in this manner. However, the assessment of her motivation made it clear that the cutting was done to appear cool.)

You can see now that this is a powerful technique. It is like planting a splinter in a kid's brain and letting him go over and over it again. You do not need to forcibly plant it. Just saying it consistently will get your adolescent to consider it. It is why I am so careful about the words I choose when discussing things with adolescents.

Many times I have adolescents who tell me that school is a waste of time. Arguing with adolescents around this concept usually results in frustration for both parties. However, using frames is a better communication mechanism in this situation. I often tell kids that some people do not graduate from high school. If you choose this route there are some things you should do now. "First of all, learn what the term supersize means and know how to apply it to drinks and fries. Also study the difference between ketchup and mustard so that when some 14 year-old tells you what to do you can hop right on it. After all, that kid is your boss when you are working. You should enjoy that quite a bit. Congratulations."

Frames can also be used for the positive. Positive frames can be put around behaviors you want to see increase. Whenever I see a kid who is struggling in school, and he does something to change it, I suggest he is a warrior and has shown that 'warrior' mentality by doing something hard and painful but important. I had a young girl who missed going out with her friends on a Friday evening to go to bed early in order to be involved with a school project on Saturday. That is a sacrifice for an adolescent. She was a Leader.

I also let kids know that they can achieve these frames, if they perform certain behaviors. For instance, when I provide therapy, I may say to an adolescent, "I treat lots of adolescents and have to decide how mature they are. The more mature a kid is, the more I treat him like an adult, and the more decisions he can make. The less mature kids get kiddy therapy. I make this assessment by seeing how well you can manage getting along in your life. Let's take a look this week at how you do with your chores, and parents, and school and then decide if you are more like an adult (positive frame) or a little kid (negative frame)". Again, he can do what he wants, but I guarantee you he wants to be seen more as an adult than a kiddy.

Let's look at three specific cases where re-framing really allowed patients to look at things differently.

Jason's (age 9) parents brought him to see me because he was always whining and crying and complaining. When I met him he seemed like a nice, funny kid who had a tendency for whining. During our discussions he related he had a 4 year-old cousin (Abbie) who was always crying and whining etc. (which would be developmentally appropriate for that age). This drove him crazy. Here was the frame. Although he loved his cousin, he did not want to act like her (after all she was 4). He also fancied himself a man's man and wanted me to know he was tough. We fashioned together a very easy chart where we listed behaviors which were 'Manning Up' (not crying, not complaining, when he fell he got right back up, taking care of his own things, etc). We also had a list called 'Abbie Behaviors' which included whining, crying, complaining, etc. We put the large board on the wall at his home and whenever he started to whine or cry his mom or dad would get out the marker and start to put a check under 'Abbie Behaviors'. Wow did that stop him in his tracks. They also took time to catch him being good ('Manning Up' in his terminology) and wrote those down as they happened. Talk about getting it. He would come in each week with a list of 'Manning Up' examples and expound on them. He began to see himself as someone who does not complain and whine and he was discharged soon afterward. Simple frame, powerful results.

John was a 17 year-old senior in high school. He had been in frequent verbal altercations with his mother to the point where she believed he had an anger problem. When I spoke with John about this he stated he wanted his mom 'off his back'. We both agreed he was doing quite well in life so she decided to coach him less. This significantly reduced the arguments (and a great example of how when the parent is a part of the problem and changes, the child gets better immediately – nice job Mom). Then John came in and was able to tell me he felt disrespected when he heard the word 'no' and that his own reaction was concerning to him. How did he come to that insight? He told me that since his mom had been 'bugging' him less he saw his part of the problem. We then talked about John's emotional maturity level. We agreed that compared to his peers he was at about the 80th percentile. More emotionally mature than most, not as emotionally mature as all. I told him that this assessment seemed accurate to me. In addition, what he was telling me about his level of self-control and impulse control did not jive with the rest of his emotional maturity level. He stated he had not seen it that way, but agreed. In order to continue to mature we need to control ourselves when things do not go our way. I asked him if he wanted to try this and he enthusiastically said yes. Thus we agreed that his homework would be to let me know when those times came up, and to let me know how he controlled his temper. He came back two weeks later and was very proud of himself. He said there had been two incidents where he normally would have 'lost it', but he reminded himself that he was more emotionally mature than this and went about his business. The frame he had in his head (to be emotionally mature means controlling myself) made all the difference to him.

This works for adults as well. One of my 17 year-olds was named Shelley. Shelley's parents were divorced and she was supposed to visit her dad every other weekend. The problem for Shelley was that her dad did not pay attention to her. Rather, he drank all day and either watched sports or went out with his friends. Shelley told her dad she would not be going over to his house again until this stopped. The dad blew a gasket. He told me that Shelley was not going to be disrespectful to him and that he would not tolerate it. The frame he viewed Shelley's talk with him in was one of disrespect.

When I sat with him I told him he was a lucky man. He seemed confused by this. I told him I had a lot of experience in this matter and often times adolescents will just stop coming over, never offering any explanation. Shelley's sitting and talking to her dad was a tremendous sign of respect. Not only that, Shelley had offered her dad a wonderful GIFT. At 17.5 years old no court order will make a relationship between Dad and daughter better. They would have to build it themselves. In Shelley's case, she had just given her dad the KEY to the relationship. Shelley wanted a sober dad who would do things with her. What a gift. Now her dad knew exactly how to build a relationship with his daughter. If he did not use the key then the relationship would probably flounder. That decision was up to the dad. He thanked me, telling me he had not thought of it like that. The frame was one of loving her dad, not disrespecting him. The dad did use the key, and I am happy to say their relationship improved dramatically.

REVIEW

1. Frames are the context in which we place behavior. Used in this manner they can be a very powerful influence on behavior.

2. If you want your child to act in a certain manner make sure he sees that his behavior is valued and that your judgments of him positively change when he acts in this manner.

3. To reduce the frequency of a behavior, make sure you place it in a negative, unattractive frame.

4. Very few kids want to be judged negatively. By placing frames around behaviors you allow your child to actually shape how they will be viewed.

5. Frames are very powerful. I will list 6 frames that you can use most times.

Positive Frames:

- People with internal fortitude do that.
- That's a sign of maturity.
- Champions do that.
- Smart people act like that.
- That's called being a leader.
- That's something an older kid would do (for a younger child).

Negative Frames:

- Immature people tend to do that.
- Most people see that as shameful.
- People must think that guy is ignorant.
- People pity people like that.
- Little babies do things like X (for younger kids).
- Wow that kid is acting like a baby (for younger kids).

CHAPTER 7

UNDERSTAND YOUR POWER

(YOUR REACTIONS AND WHAT THEY MEAN)

Quite often I am approached by a parent who will ask "What should I do if I find out my child is taking drugs"? My answer is, "It really depends". 'Taking drugs' is not a unitary concept. Your reaction should differ depending on what you have found.

Let's looks at an example from my practice.

Parent: Doc, what should I do now that I have found out my kid is using drugs?

Dr. Matt: Tell me about it.

Parent: Well, I caught him and his friends smoking pot last Saturday night in our basement.

Dr. Matt: When the kids got caught, what did they say?

Parent: They said one of their friends at school had given it to them and they wanted to try it because they had never done it before.

Now when I say taking drugs can mean many different things, just think of your own parental reaction to the above scenario. Now let's consider if we changed dope to heroin, and 'trying it' to 'I have been using it regularly for 6 months'. I bet your reaction to 'drugs' would be very different..... And it should be.

Understand that your reaction is one of the things that will imprint on your adolescent. In the first case, I would choose a very measured, problem solving approach focusing on why this is not going to be OK in your home, etc. There may or may not be calls to the other adolescents homes, but if it happens again, count on calls.

The second scenario would be followed by a detox center and a stint in rehab. There should be far more precautions and ramifications for this 'drug usage' along with very firm limits for the adolescent.

Using the same reaction, especially anger, for everything renders it meaningless. If you get as upset with clothes on the floor as you do at slamming heroin, of course your child is going to devalue your response. It is important to teach kids the difference between mistakes and dangerous situations. Yes, they are both mistakes but one is far more egregious than the other.

Take Paula, an A student, who, in the course of one week, got a D on a test (which she was really upset about) and a DUI (also upset). The two "mistakes" are vastly different and should have vastly different consequences. A 'D' is meaningless in life and can easily be erased, changed, modified, etc. Killing yourself or someone else in a car while drunk is never going to change. This is life altering and life threatening.

Make sure as a parent that your responses to these situations differ significantly. In this way, there are clear clues for your child, which tell her what is a mistake and what is intolerable.

BE WISE WITH HOUSE RULES

Here is a good place to discuss one important tenet of a home contract (I will cover 15 rules for contracts in the next chapter). Often I get parents who come to me with their home contract. These parents are usually very diligent and have one or two typed pages with signatures at the end. On the pages are between 20 and 30 rules. How would you like to go to work and have 20-30 rules thrust upon you? You would not, and you would probably find subtle ways to rebel. Hallelujah – your adolescent is like you.

I tell parents they should probably have 3 or 4 rules on a contract that are mandated. The rest we will talk about. The rules could be 'we talk to each other with respect', 'we do not use illicit drugs in our home', 'we never stay out all night without informing the family where we are', etc. These are essential rules for the family to function.

All the rest is just stuff you can discuss and contract on a week-to-week basis. Having so few rules tells your child there are not 25 things of equal importance in our home. There are 3-4 basic rules and the rest we will work out as a family. This is a lot easier to understand and draws an important distinction between rules which must be kept, and those we can work on.

In addition, parents will often tell me they do not know what to use as punishers and rewards. While I will cover this more when I discuss Pendulum Rewards, this mindset is one of those, which has been foisted on parents. Your adolescent has virtually nothing without you providing it for them. Anything you provide to your adolescent is done out of caring for that child. All the electronics, computers, access to televisions, rides to places, etc. are from your generosity. Instead of providing these at no cost, perhaps a number of these things should be earned. They all take effort on your part. Why not make them contingent on a little effort from your adolescent. Certainly a ride to a friend's house for a sleep over must be worth at least one chore. The difficulty is that many parents have been brainwashed into believing they have to provide this to their adolescent. When in reality your adolescent lives off the generosity of your good graces.

Remember, you are the power in your home. Use it wisely.

DEAL BREAKERS

One of my favorite stories occurred when I was the Clinical Supervisor of Services at a large mental health facility. I was quite young at the time, playing hockey, and wore my hair down the middle of my back. Certainly I did not look like your average doctor, but I was well respected and did good work. One day I received a phone call. I was just starting my private practice and one of my colleagues had referred a case to me.

The mom called me. I asked if this was a crisis or if we could schedule an appointment in the next few days. The mom told me she felt it was a crisis. This piqued my interest so I asked what the problem was with her son. She said "You should see his hair; I mean it is over his collar". I scheduled her immediately. I also called my colleague and asked what he thought. He said that this mom was quite critical of her son. This was just the latest sign to her that he would not turn out well. She needed a wake-up call since he was an excellent kid, athlete, etc. He thought 'seeing me' (literally) might add a sense of perspective to the mom.

The day of the appointment was quite humorous. I came down the hall with my very long hair blowing in the breeze and saw a mom with her 16 year-old. He was clean cut as far as I could see. I stopped and asked if they were waiting for someone. She said, "Yes, Dr. Duggan is going to see my son. He comes highly recommended and we need someone to talk to David". I see I said, "Well thank you for the compliment, I am Dr. Duggan and so why don't you and I go to my office and talk". You should have seen her eyes. To this day I still laugh as I do when I think of David's smirk. What was even funnier was when I asked why she was there. She just could not bring herself to let me know that his hair touching his collar meant he was destined to be a loser.

As we got to the office she asked me again "Are you the Dr. Duggan who is the Clinical Supervisor over all these units?" "I am," I said. "I am the one who came highly recommended. Now what is the problem?" She was now embarrassed to speak so we spent a good deal of time discussing the difference between what is really important and what is really not important. One of the foundations of development is that all healthy kids rebel. If you are lucky enough to have a kid who does it with his hair, or his room, or a beard, then you have been truly blessed because there are many forms of rebelliousness which are far more dangerous and destructive.

I suggested that this particular mom look at the 4 major areas of David's life – his family relationships, his peer relationships, how he is doing in school (including extracurriculars), and how he feels about himself. If these areas are not showing cracks then her son is probably doing well. She conceded that he was doing fine in school and athletics. He was respectful to his family members, and was well liked by his peers. He seemed to have a pretty positive attitude, DESPITE HIS HAIR TOUCHING HIS COLLAR. In other words, he was functioning not just well, but successfully.

I saw David a few times and assured his mom that she had done something right because he was a great kid. I asked her to allow him to have his hair how he wants it as long as he continues to achieve in the areas of his life which are truly important. I ran into David some years later, when he was in college, and we had a good laugh about the meeting. On a positive note, he stated that his mom 'got it' and never bugged him about inconsequential stuff again. We ended our encounter with his sharing that he was about to graduate from college with a degree in engineering.

This is why when I speak to parents there are many topics where I will not help them. Among them: hair, room cleanliness (with the caveat of food in the room which can be a health hazard), eating the right foods, etc. These are issues which resolve themselves over time, and which need not be managed.

Instead of focusing on minutiae or everything your adolescent does, parents should have 4 or 5 DEAL BREAKER RULES. Rules where they will not tolerate a violation. These should include such things as no drugs, we respect each other, you attend and work at your only job – school, no physical violence against family members, and do not put yourself in harms way. All the rest is minutia which you can deal with.

Granted the rules will vary by family and environment. For instance, I see a lot of single parents in my practice. Like it or not, it is tougher to raise a kid alone than with two parents. This is less a moral stance and more one of practicality. Many of the single parents I see want to discipline and monitor as if there are two parents. This is not possible and can lead to a lot of disappointment and resentment. If you are a single parent, it is important to acknowledge this and to realize that your deal breakers may be quite a bit different from a family with two active parents. One of my single parents was wracked with guilt because one of her deal breakers was insisting that her 16 year-old child watch her 7 year-old until she got home from work. She correctly surmised that had her husband not passed away this would not fall on the 16 year-old. However her guilt over it was self-generated. The family unit needed this adjustment and the 16 year-old was quite capable of doing this. It is important to look at your situation when creating rules and not to buy into the one-size-fits-all mentality.

Similarly, if your family farms and lives off the profits from your farm, then working on that farm becomes a deal breaker.

Again, kids should be aware of what rules are negotiable and which are not and parents should be prepared to discipline accordingly.

TEACHING VS. BERATING

Let's talk about jumping all over your adolescent for an error versus helping him see and correct the error. One of the major airlines incorporated an alarm system into their reservation agents' computers. The alarm would sound whenever the agent made an error, which needed correcting. The airlines incorrectly believed that the quicker the sound, the more effective it would be. So, whenever an error occurred, the alarm sounded almost simultaneously with the incorrect key being hit on the keyboard. Since the sound occurred before the agent even had a chance to think and correct the error, it was often startling and unsettling. In fact, what the airline found was that the agents became so frustrated at the alarm that they actually slowed their pace down to a crawl just to keep from hearing the sound. This was extremely inefficient and the system was scrapped.

The same is true for your adolescent. Helping them to cognitively understand their error is important. If they are able to see it and change it, it is less likely to happen in the future. Parents who hover and then pounce often end up producing kids who are too afraid to take any kind of risk since this will lead to a noxious outcome.

A 15 year-old boy named Brad came to see me. He was in big trouble. He had wanted to ask a girl out and had approached her at school. He asked a very inappropriate, sexual-in-nature, question. His parents got a call from the girl's parents who were understandably upset. Brad's parents wanted to know how much they should punish Brad. Their ideas ranged from grounding for six months to placing him in boarding school for a year. After hearing from his distraught parents, I assumed I would meet an over-masculinized, aggressive male who was learning to be a predator. Instead, I found a confused and upset adolescent who knew he had made a major mistake. As we spoke, it became clear that Brad was no predator. He was socially immature and trying to make 'cool' contact. He had received most of his training from the Internet and saw this as a way to have peers see him as cool and perhaps get a girlfriend. He could not have been more incorrect on either count.

When we spoke of the response that the girl might have to his query, he cried and stated he did not consider this. This was a good example of a kid who needed an arm around him, understanding that he was lonely and trying to reach out. He also needed some direct teaching on how to interact with peers without placing himself in an even worse social position. I suggested a small, but firm punishment along with a lot of social skills training. I worked with Brad for about a year and he did quite well. By the time we ended therapy, he had developed a couple of close friends and was doing well. I ran into Brad about 3 years later. I did not recognize him because he had physically matured so much. He was in college, had a girlfriend for the past year and was studying business.

    Will, a precocious 19 year-old, was away at college. Will was a very smart young man, but had not really worked up to his full potential in high school. However he did get into college and was happy to be there. Unfortunately, bad habits such as being undisciplined about studying tend to follow adolescents. Will found himself about to get expelled from school due to poor performance. He had written a very complete note to the Dean of the School accepting full responsibility for his behavior -even though I could see that some things had been out of his control. He acknowledged his behavioral pattern, and provided a full outline of the steps he had taken, and would continue to take, to be a proud graduate of the school. I was amazed at the maturity of the letter and at the aggressive steps he had taken to assure he would be allowed back into the school. He was invited to speak to the Dean and his father was also asked to attend. The Dean threw his letter in the trash and tore into Will. His father was taken aback by the harshness of the meeting and stated that had he known how cruel this man would be, he would not have allowed Will to attend the meeting. Will was dismissed from the school.

    The father called to ask me if he should discipline his son. We spoke about where Will was and where he had come from. He acknowledged how Will had accepted full responsibility for his behavior and implemented a plan to rectify it. These are the things we want to see from adolescents who are progressing into adulthood. We agreed that Will needed an arm around him and a pep talk. The dad still acknowledged that Will put himself in this tenuous position, but he also let Will know he was proud of how he tried to dig himself out. What Will needed now was understanding and support and his father was very good at providing both. There are few things more powerful than the understanding and love of a parent. Will attended another school for one year. He did quite well and re-applied to the old school. Although both his father and I cringed at this, you have to admire the determination of this young man. He was re-admitted and will be graduating soon.

I know when parents are in the middle of a storm, it is hard to decide what to do, but there are often issues where understanding and teaching are far better tools than punishment. A parent's love is second to none. There are times when a hug says much more than any words or other actions.

LEARNED HELPLESSNESS

The last concept to share (and to warn you about) is that of learned helplessness. One of the themes of this book is that it is better to teach your adolescents to take controlled risks than to have someone who is too afraid to take any risks. While there are numerous reasons why a child may be afraid to take risks, one may be that they have *learned to not act* via learned helplessness.

This concept has been explored for many years and entails teaching someone that his behavior will have no effect. The original studies focused on placing a dog in a large box with a screen splitting the box in two. The side the dog was on would be wired to shock the dog. When this happened the dog would jump to avoid the shock but would hit the glass and fall back on the electrified side. Within a relatively short period of time, even when the barrier was removed and escape was possible, the dog would no longer attempt to escape and just accept the shock. The dog had been taught that his behavior made no difference and that he would be punished regardless of what he did. He had learned to be helpless. Surprisingly, this phenomenon can be induced quite quickly.

When a parent is overbearing and extremely harsh and persistent, adolescents will often shut down and not try. This kind of 'teaching' can lead to lifelong problems. As an aside, I have also seen this in marriages, which have lost all compassion and love; and where one spouse is beaten down to the point of complete submissiveness. The beaten down spouse has 'learned' that his behavior has no effect, so why do anything.

REVIEW

1. Using the same reaction for everything renders it meaningless. For example, although leaving your room messy and drug usage are both problems for adolescents, your reaction to these two problems should be quite different.

2. Home Contracts – Make 3 to 5 rules which are extremely important to your home and which are not negotiable. The rest of the rules should be flexible and negotiable. Remember that many of the things you give to your adolescent (rides, electronics, etc.) can be used as rewards or consequences.

3. Deal Breakers – These are the rules in your home, which are not negotiable. There should be a few of these and your kids should know that if these are broken, there will be swift consequences with no discussion.

4. Teaching versus Berating – In adolescence, when a child makes a foolish error and does not understand why it is an error, it is imperative that parents take the time to help their child cognitively understand what happened and why.

5. Learned Helplessness – If you are too overbearing, your child will learn to be meek and timid. It is important you balance discipline with love and teaching.

CHAPTER 8

BUILDING A HOME CONTRACT: 15 HOT TIPS

I am including this chapter because contracts are one of the most poorly understood concepts in parenting. Parents use contracts all the time with their children. What is a contract? They are simply If/Then statements that allow children/adolescents to understand and predict what outcome will result from their behaviors. They can be simple and small such as, "If you eat your vegetables, you will get dessert", or, "If you clean your room, you may go out and play". Or, as your children grow, they can be more sophisticated and focus on more important behaviors, e.g., "If you have a B average, you can apply for your learner's permit".

The idea of a contract seems easy enough, but it is actually quite a complicated task to do properly. There are many nuances to creating and applying a contract. The challenges increase as the sophistication of the contract grows. If they are not done well, they can lead to frustration for both parents and the adolescent. Therefore, below are 15 points to keep in mind when developing a contract.

CONTRACTS ARE ABOUT DECISION-MAKING

Please read this again. Contracts are about teaching adolescent to make decisions. There they are NOT ABOUT CHANGING BEHAVIOR. Behavioral change comes AFTER your adolescent realizes and experiences the consequences of his behavior. I cannot tell you the number of times parents tell me that the contract is not working because the adolescent's behavior did not immediately change. I then ask if they applied the consequences, and I hear they have not because they did not want to apply them in the first place. The contract ONLY tells your adolescent WHAT will happen WHEN they make certain decisions. For instance, it is fine if your adolescent does not take out the trash, he will just not have access to his computer for the next 24 hours. That is a choice and a consequence. Similarly, the computer is available if the garbage is out by 7 PM. That is a choice and a consequence. Please remember behavior change is secondary to learning.

START WITH SMALL, DEFINED TASKS

In order to prep your adolescent for the use of a contract I suggest starting with just one or two behaviors which are easily defined and which you are going to reward and/or punish. Yes, that means for the first week many items will go unconsequenced, but this will change as you add to the contract over time. It does no good to overload an adolescent as they are learning how this works. In addition, if they start to become successful at the behaviors you are rewarding, they often want more behaviors and rewards. In fact, one of my biggest problems with using contracts is siblings begin to insist that they deserve to have a contract as well. After all, the behaviors which are rewarded, are clearly outlined and usually relatively easy to do.

CREATE CONTRACTS BEFORE A PROBLEM

Too many times parents wait until a problem occurs and then feel lost as to what to do. Most parents are well aware of what areas they are going to experience problems in with their adolescent. The beauty of a contract is that your responses to these problems are pre-designed so you do not need to decide on them at the crisis point. You have been clear with your adolescent and now you are just a scorekeeper wondering which decision he will make and what consequence (positive or negative) your adolescent will choose.

CLEARLY DEFINE BEHAVIORS/TIMES

When I see contracts with words like moral behavior, trust, good behaviors, good grades, etc., I cringe. Why? Because these have no concrete definition. For instance is 'good grades' a 3.0 or above? A 2.8 or above? A 2.5 or above? Define the criteria so anyone, anywhere could enforce it. For instance, 'moral behavior' might become sharing with someone three or more times a day, etc. These are things your child or adolescent understands and can do.

Likewise, specify time when designing a contract. For instance, if the behavior to be consequenced is doing the dishes, please let your adolescent know what time you will check (say 7:30 PM). This keeps those silly arguments from occurring about doing the dishes at midnight. In addition, have a standard clock you use (like the one hanging in the kitchen). That way everyone is not looking at different timepieces.

Remember you are just keeping score once the options are set up.

QUICK PAYOFFS

In psychology we call these 'payoffs at the point of performance'. If you want to experience the highest appreciation and connection between a behavior and reward, provide the reward when and where the behavior is performed. For instance, if a child understands that when he obeys his mom, he gets a piece of candy, then carry that candy around with you and pay him when he obeys you. 'Owing' a kid is always a bad idea and dilutes the association between behavior and reward. You can see now why telling your adolescent you will take him to Disney World in 9 months if he gets a 3.0 does almost nothing for his motivation. It is much better to tell him you will take him to the batting cages every week that he brings home a grade check with a 3.0 on it.

REAL CONSEQUENCES WORK BEST

You know what really motivates kids to get home on time? Changing the curfew to a later time. You know what motivates a kid to get his car home on time? More car time. You know what motivates kids to get ready by bedtime? Later bedtime. When you can use the child or adolescent's environment to provide rewards and punishment you will find adolescents work very hard for them. The idea that you have to pay off with giant motivators is untrue. Kids work for what THEY value.

PENDULUM REWARDS AND PUNISHERS

This is covered in the chapter 'Adolescents Must Be Made Responsible For Their Own Behavior'. However, it fits well here so a brief review is in order. When you can use something as BOTH a reward and punisher you have found a pendulum. There are so many in adolescence it is hard not to find them. So let's look at one.

Driver's licenses are great pendulums. When your child is acting appropriately, he has access to this perk. When he is not, he loses it for a period of time. Feel free to substitute computers, cell phones, television, car, time with peers, etc. for driver's license.

DON'T BE AFRAID TO CHANGE THE REWARDS AND PUNISHERS

Sometimes the things you and/or your adolescent have chosen just do not bring enough enjoyment or pain from which to learn. For instance, if I gain a penny when I am on time or lose one when I am late, I may not really care if I am on time. In these cases, experiment with other rewards and punishers. Adolescents often have great ideas that will work for them. Throw out the outrageous ideas, i.e. $100 a week allowance, new car, etc., and try the realistic ones, i.e. a later curfew, more computer time, etc.

TOKENS

There are times when an adolescent wants to work for bigger goals. If you have decided on this, then tell your adolescent you will pay him off with tokens for behavior. These can be saved and accrued for a larger reward if they earn enough. For instance, you may develop a chart where your adolescent can earn 500 tokens (chips, credits, etc.) per day. If he wants to earn a big payoff (like a video game, a day snowboarding, etc.), then he must save up 10000 tokens (possibly in a month). Token systems are good for sophisticated adolescents and large rewards. They are a lot harder to manage but if your adolescent will work for these goals, they can be useful.

SAY WHAT YOU MEAN AND MEAN WHAT YOU SAY

A huge problem can ensue with contracts when parents agree to do something, but do not mean it. This is a MAJOR problem. For instance, if your child has earned a reward and now it is inconvenient (or more than you wanted to do), your adolescent will learn you do not follow your word. I suggest that all parents follow through. If the contract has to change later, then sit down and do so. Likewise, if your child earns the punisher and now you do not want to apply it, your adolescent will accurately realize that the contract has little to no meaning. This realization can be quite destructive to the parent-adolescent relationship. Therefore, I always review the contract with each parent until I have assurance from BOTH parents that the contract will be followed.

EXCUSES, EXCUSES, EXCUSES

Simply put – there are no excuses. Adolescents almost always attempt to explain any behavior leading to a punisher with excuses. Some of them will be brilliant. I suggest that you let your adolescent know that although you will listen to him, his excuses will not change your agreement. Therefore, if a friend would not drive your adolescent home, he has still missed curfew. If his cell phone went dead, he still did not answer as required, etc. Even good decisions sometimes result in negative outcomes. That does not mean parents should not applaud the good behavior (and they can reward it in some manner if they choose), it is just that the contract (the word of the parent and adolescent) should be heeded and applied.

IT'S OK TO COMMISERATE

I tell parents this is about decision-making and sometimes your adolescent will make some poor decisions. This is not a war, nor an opportunity to shame your adolescent. Often adolescent decisions will result in punishment and missed opportunities. When I get parents who are so emotionally involved with their adolescents that the parent goes through the same pain as the child, I grow concerned. I strongly suggest that parents take a step back, commiserate with their adolescent and move forward with their own lives. For instance, if an adolescent had the choice to arrive home by 7PM to view a favorite movie with the family, it is OK to commiserate if they are late. It is fine to say "Wow, what a bummer you are late. We were looking forward to sharing this with you, but we understand sometimes time just flies by. This is a bummer for us as well as we will really miss you. We will check in on you after we watch the movie. We love you and hope it goes better for you tomorrow." Then go watch the movie.

WORK THE CONTRACT

I often have parents who tell me "The contract is not working". When I ask them why, they say their adolescent is not following it. Since part of any good contract is sitting down with your adolescent at the end of the day and reviewing their behavior within the contract, I ask what is being said. Often I find parents are not doing this. They think the contract will magically work on its own. WRONG. Your adolescent will care about the contract as much as you do. If it is not worth reviewing each day it is probably not worth instituting. You should sit down with him each evening and spend 3-5 minutes reviewing the contract, behaviors, and consequences. He will see this is a vital document to you and one that will take center stage in his freedoms.

CHANGES IN THE CONTRACT

No one gets it totally right the first time. However, I suggest that parents do not change the contract until a set date. Perhaps every Sunday night you get together to discuss it and make any changes. Then you live with the changes throughout the week. Sure there will be times when the rewards are too high or the punishment too low, but you can live with that for a week. There is no changing again until Sunday night. Again, your adolescent will realize this is a pretty important meeting and that complaining during the week does little good.

WHAT SHOULD YOU REWARD

I saved this for last since this is one of the great debates in parenting today. We hear all the time 'why should we reward an adolescent for things he should be doing'. The answer is BECAUSE IT WORKS.

Let me give you an example about shaping behavior by rewarding mammals. Shamu is the killer whale at Sea World who jumps about 20 feet in the air and over a bar held out by a trainer. How do they get that great animal to perform such a feat? Do you think they just watch until she does it herself one day? No. Do they put the bar on top of the water and wait for her to pass over it? No. Believe it or not they start by putting the bar on the BOTTOM of the pool and rewarding her whenever she passes over it. That's right; they reward her for something at which she CANNOT FAIL. Little by little they raise the bar until eventually she is performing this great feat. While it is amazing, it starts by rewarding her for something she cannot miss.

Your adolescent works very much like this, albeit, with a small twist. There is nothing wrong with rewarding an adolescent for good grades, jobs well done, etc. In fact 'catching' your adolescent being good and rewarding him with attention, feedback, etc., is one of the most powerful teaching tools you have.

However, and this is where lots of parents trip, it is important to point out WHAT you are rewarding and WHY. This is crucial so your adolescent knows what action pays off.

It is important to let your adolescent know you are not just rewarding actions but you are rewarding persistence, effort, determination, grit, etc. These are the characteristics you want to instill in your child. These are the things you should highlight.

I often point to my diplomas on the wall and tell kids "These do not mean I am smart. What they mean is I am determined. I went to class. I handed in homework; I did what was necessary to graduate". While I may be intelligent, I earned my degrees through effort.

Which kid would you rather have, the one who gets a job from his parents and takes it for granted or the kid who fills out 50 applications and is still looking? The second will be successful and should be rewarded. Getting a job is outside his control, but his effort is not.

Talk about being rewarded for things you should do, how would you like your employer to say you had an average day today so you don't get paid? You are just doing what you should do.

Too many parents mix up results with effort. You will have many more victories (and failures) if you are willing to keep trying. Effort, especially persistent effort, should be rewarded.

This is why I love John Wooden's books. He often speaks about how one becomes successful. His recipe has to do with doing your best. He speaks glowingly about games he lost where his team played up to their peak potential. He speaks remorsefully about games his teams won where they did not play their best. He does not value those games and sees them as opportunities lost. Likewise, in practice he did not keep score. He felt people played to the score rather than playing to the best of their abilities.

The only real losers are those who lose their will to try and persevere. They are doomed to accept what others give them, all the while never finding out what they could have earned.

The process of instilling these characteristics comes through parents' appreciation of these skills. This is what separates those who will succeed from those who will not.

I will end this chapter by noting two things I have in my office. One is a large sign I received from a hockey arena. It directs PARTICIPANTS to walk to the left and SPECTATORS to the right. I always want my kids to veer left. As Teddy Roosevelt said: "It is not the critic who counts, nor the man who points out where the strong man tumbled, nor where the doers of deeds could have done them better. On the contrary, the credit belongs to the man who is actually in the arena – whose vision is marred by the dust and sweat and blood; who strives valiantly; who errs and comes up again and again; who knows the great devotions, the great enthusiasms; who at best knows in the end the triumph of high achievement. However, if he fails, if he falls, at least he fails while daring greatly so his place shall never be with those cold and timid souls who know neither victory nor defeat."

The second reminder I have in my office was written by Tom Callahan of the Washington Post around the time of the Olympics. It speaks to effort, courage and determination. "In a basement somewhere, a canoeist has converted a small coal bin into a stagnant river. He's crouched on one knee intermittently paddling nowhere. The sloshing is a night sound of the neighborhood, a beguiling mystery to the neighbors. A roller skate wedged beneath his forward foot simulates the rocking of the boat. Old mirrors of every shape, rescued from dressers and garage sales, are suspended all around him. In their reflections his technique can be checked against the home movies he has taken of the Romanians and the Swedes. He can't win and he doesn't even know about merchandising. He's just a hero."

Being a hero in the real world has little to do with winning and losing, effort and determination pave the way.

REVIEW

1. Over my 25 years in practice, contracting is one of the areas where I see parents make the most mistakes. Contracts appear easy on the surface but are often challenging to create and implement successfully. When contracts are not done well they can lead to extreme frustration for both the parents and the child/adolescent.

2. When developing and implementing a contract there are many things to keep in mind. This chapter briefly outlines 15 of those things.

3. Among the most important things to remember is that you should reward effort, diligence, hard work, persistence and all other human qualities that are under our control and define us.

4. It is not just OK, but smart, to reward your adolescent for behaviors you want them to continue, even if your adolescent is doing those behaviors anyway. This often entails catching your adolescent (or child) being good and letting him know you appreciate it.

CHAPTER 9

WHAT MAKES A KID SUCCESSFUL:

EMOTIONAL QUOTIENT (EQ) OVER INTELLECTUAL QUOTIENT (IQ)

This is one of the most difficult concepts for parents to grasp even though they see it every day, everywhere. IQ is important as a starting point for successful people. Obviously, if your IQ is 70 it will most likely place some limits on where you can go. However, IQ does not seem determinative of where you will go or what you can attain.

IQ is like a foundation. You need it to build upon. However, IQ can't really get you anywhere alone. To build a life you need a lot more, and most of it is EQ.

What is EQ? It stands for Emotional Quotient. The book which brought EQ to the forefront of American culture, was titled *Emotional Quotient: Why It Can Matter More Than IQ*, written by Daniel Goleman, Ph.D. He suggested there were five main domains that encompass EQ. These are: knowing one's emotions (self-awareness), managing emotions (handling emotions), motivating oneself (self-control, stifling impulsiveness), recognizing emotions in others (empathy), and handling relationships.

Although the idea of being able to assess and understand what is happening emotionally with yourself and those around you has been around a long time, this book showed what a powerful force this can be. Up until then it was assumed that the most powerful business people in America were those with the highest IQs. This was tested when researchers looked at the IQ's of many of these people. When the data came in, the results were quite surprising and led these researchers to coin the term EQ. The data showed that the most powerful business people had IQ's, which were above average but certainly not in the genius range. So what accounted for their ascendancy to the highest levels of American business? It was their EQs. The people who became leaders had excellent people skills. They knew how to read people and events and were often characterized as easy to get along with, someone who can bring people together, a team player, someone you wanted to interact with and who could help gel a meeting. Others around them wanted them to succeed because they were well liked and good at getting things done in a manner which made everyone feel appreciated. Yes, they had to be bright, but there are literally hundreds of bright people in these companies. What separated the leaders was their Emotional Quotients.

If you have read the best seller *Outliers*, you have seen the research performed by Lewis Terman, Ph.D. He was fascinated with gifted children and his research focused on following a group of them throughout their lives. He believed that because of their high IQ's these children would grow into young men and women who would rise to the highest levels in society and be difference makers. As with the EQ study, he found that although their IQ's placed them at the very highest levels of intelligence, most of their lives were quite mundane. Thus, IQ itself does not seem to correlate with success. It is a necessary component but not sufficient by itself.

Bell Labs did a review of their engineers in an attempt to see what variables correlated with the most success. Again what they found was that success at Bell had little correlation with IQ. Rather those engineers deemed most friendly, most able to build consensus and who were most liked and appreciated by their peers, received the highest honors and promotions. Again, EQ seems to be the variable that trumps all the rest.

P.M. Forni, author of "Choosing Civility: The 25 Rules of Considerate Conduct", stated that "Social intelligence is a much more accurate predictor of success at work, in school and in life than the kind of intelligence that we measure with IQ". I could not agree more.

Now let's look at adolescence. When I was on the Board of Education, I was constantly amazed at the power that IQ testing scores held over parents. It was as if God himself had come down and given your child a score, which would cement them into a social stratum for the rest of their lives. This is still the way it is done in schools. Many schools actually 'teach to the test' now to assure higher scores.

I am so skeptical of this because I have given over 1000 IQ tests, first at Children's Hospital, then at Memorial Medical Center, and finally in my own practice. The scores have value, but nowhere near the value ascribed to them. The score is one measure, on one day, on one test. Think of everything you know about your child – are you really willing to abandon all those beliefs if the 'score' is not what was expected? People (and I mean professionals too) throw all common sense away when they see scores. They are willing to suspend everything they know if a 'score' is different from their knowledge.

A particularly scary, yet poignant, example of this happened when I was at Memorial Medical Center. We had a young lady on our unit, Kate, who was 20 years old. In all my dealings with her (over the two weeks she was in the hospital for a spinal cord injury) she was coherent, humorous, and bright. In fact she had graduated from high school in the top 15% of her class and was attending college. The perception of her on the unit was that she was a nice young lady who would do well in life.

Her family asked that she be tested. When we case-conferenced about her, I could not believe what I was hearing. The professional who had done the testing told us that Kate was functioning at the level of a first grader and we should treat her as such. No more asking her to help with her treatment or getting guidance from her. That kind of talk would only confuse her and lead to poor decisions.

As people were writing this down I interrupted and stated that the assessment must be incorrect. "If you just talk to Kate you can see she is smart, you don't need a test for that", I stated. I was told that may be true, but she is probably compensating because THE TEST SAYS she is functioning at a 7 year-old level.

I suggested we not act on this and requested the data from the test. When I reviewed it, I found that it had been scored incorrectly and that Kate had actually scored above average for her age.

It is important to remember that these are only tests and your own common sense is often at least as powerful.

It is just as silly to judge a child on one test as it would be to judge Michael Jordan on one shot, or Einstein on one foolish thought (by the way he was a poor student who received poor test scores). If the score does not fit, reassess or discard.

In a society where we put so much value on IQ, it is no wonder we hear kids describe themselves in these terms. When I hear Mary assert, "I am a 3.1", I say "No you are not, you are Mary and there is much more to you than your GPA". In fact, I often say "Your IQ is important but being a determined, self starter who gets along with others is far more important".

When I meet with families and I see that their child is at least of an average IQ, I look much more closely at EQ. This is the variable, which will be most determinative of future success.

The ability to synthesize and react to what is going on around you socially and psychologically is the entire house built on the IQ foundation. The better the skill, the bigger the house. It is crucial to teach your kids to get along well with people, work as a good teammate, control their impulses enough to make good decisions, and not be selfish.

Just think of all the successful people around you. I bet their IQs and educations vary greatly, but most, if not all, have excellent EQs and that is why they have been able to be successful in this world.

It is almost apocryphal to talk about the genius who is homeless because others have tired of him. Having played sports all my life, I can tell you that good athletes, who are cancers in the locker room (poor EQ), do not make it very far. Remember, IQ sets the table, but EQ does all the rest.

REVIEW

1. The idea that IQ is determinative of future success is firmly rooted in our culture. Unfortunately, under scientific analysis one can see that a factor far more predictive of future success is EQ – Emotional Quotient.

2. People who have a good understanding of other people, and can create environments within which others feel valued and appreciated, tend to be the people we look up to and want to be around. It is also the best predictor of future success.

3. This ability spans every facet of life. The ability to understand our environment, and the people in it, is one of the most important principles parents should teach their children and adolescents.

CHAPTER 10

WHAT IF YOUR ADOLESCENT HAS A SEVERE PSYCHIATRIC ISSUE?

Most of what I have written in this book is geared toward 'regular' adolescents. These are kids who are a pain in the rear, yet underneath it all are good kids who need some help here and there. I am including this chapter as a warning not to rely exclusively on these techniques if your child suffers from a serious psychiatric problem.

Serious psychiatric problems include, but are not limited to, severe depression, panic disorder, obsessive-compulsive disorder, bipolar disorders, all psychotic disorders, conduct disorders, substance dependency disorders, to name a few. While there are many diagnoses listed here, most adolescents do not meet the criteria for these disorders.

If you believe your child does fall into this category take him to a mental health professional and have him properly assessed. Severe psychopathology can be life threatening. Having a strong and competent treatment plan, including psychological and medical intervention, is crucial. While the skills in this book may be useful, they are not enough if the child has a severe problem. This is one of the reasons I always suggest obtaining a competent psychological assessment whenever a parent feels this may be going on with their child.

If you are not sure your child has a severe problem, examine the four areas which encompass most of their lives: their family relationships, their school behavior and grades (including extracurriculars), their social life, and how they feel about themselves. When adolescents are in psychiatric distress they will usually show cracks in at least three of these areas. Thus, I usually take a cautious approach and suggest an evaluation whenever a parent sees that at least two of these areas are suffering.

To give you an example, I had a parent call me and ask if their 19 year-old son needed a psychiatric assessment. His name was Paul and he was away at school. However, they had just seen his grade report, which had 4 incompletes and an F on it. When they called the school to inquire about his grades, they found that Paul (normally an A/B student) had not attended any of his finals (school based concern). When they called his dorm room they spoke to his roommate, who related he thought something was wrong with Paul. Paul was staying up all night and seemed to not make a lot of sense when he spoke. He also had an idea that he was going to start a shoe company on campus to "Put Nike in its place". His roommate noted that he and a number of Paul's friends were becoming increasingly concerned (socially based concern). Lastly, Paul had not spoken to his family in over two weeks. This was odd since they had a standing agreement to speak twice a week. The family had called him repeatedly but he had not responded (family based concern). I suggested they call the campus mental health center and have someone go over and interview Paul as soon as possible. They called me back the next day stating that they had taken my advice. Paul had been hospitalized for suffering a bi-polar break (he had a psychotic episode). The ending to this story was quite positive. Paul was stabilized in the hospital and received competent psychiatric treatment. He was able to re-involve himself in school and is on target to graduate.

Amy was a 16 year-old girl who was brought to my office by her parents. She had always been a very pleasant, somewhat shy, young lady. She was a B/C student and had a desire to attend college. This past semester she had been repeatedly skipping school. Consequently her grades were very poor and her counselor called her parents concerned about Amy (school based concern). Her parents noted that Amy had 4 or 5 best friends since middle school. They noted that they had not seen these girls in many months (socially based concern). The parents noted it was like they did not know who this girl was in their home. What was once a close family had disintegrated into Amy coming home, hiding in her room, and barely interacting with either parent (family based concern). When I saw Amy, she was depressed and angry. She was upset with herself (Problems With How She Views Herself). Given my past experience, it was not hard to see that Amy had been abusing drugs for the past 4-6 months. Her usage started out as a social thing and had escalated into daily usage (including skipping school to get high). Fortunately, Amy was motivated to change, which she did over the course of therapy. I applaud her parents for seeing this was not just an adolescent problem, but also a major problem for which seeking psychiatric help was beneficial.

REVIEW

1. The techniques described in this book are beneficial ideas for MOST adolescents. However, if your child/adolescent is suffering from a severe psychiatric problem, then you should insist that they receive a complete psychological assessment and treatment when necessary.

2. When making this assessment it is best to get the input of a trained professional (your pediatrician, psychologist, psychiatrist, other mental health professional, etc).

3. As a rule of thumb I ask parents to examine the four areas of an adolescent's life which encompass most of what they do - their school life (grades and extracurriculars); their home life; their social life; and how they feel about themselves. If there are cracks in two of these areas, I suggest an evaluation. If there are cracks in three or four areas, then an evaluation is absolutely necessary.

10 THINGS PARENTS SHOULD DO

CHAPTER 1

LISTEN …….AND THEY WILL TELL YOU EXACTLY WHO THEY ARE

LISTENING

The act of listening consists of hearing what someone is saying and attending to its meaning. There it is – listening. The definition makes it sound soooo easy. Why, then, are there so many times that people become frustrated because, 'You aren't listening to me!'?. Well, one of the reasons is because the definition is actually two skills wrapped together. The hearing part is quite easy. One needs only to open one's ears and you can hear. The second part, attending to one's meaning, is much harder.

Let me give you an example from way back in the 1980's when I was doing my dissertation. Part of my dissertation consisted of videotaping mock juries deliberating on a case which was presented to them. My dissertation had to do with how jurors perceived children giving testimony. This came out of a discussion with the Buffalo DA's office where the DAs were losing numerous cases that had children as key witnesses. They were interested in finding out why (I will not go into my findings here, although they can be found in the book, *"Perspectives on Children's Testimony"* printed by Springer-Verlag).

When my team broke down the videos, something unexpected, but interesting, happened. Although we were all watching the same videotapes, we were having trouble assessing just what the jurors meant. It was very common for two team members, who saw the same tape, to have quite different interpretations of what a juror 'meant'. This happened so often that one of my colleagues used the same tapes to do her dissertation on language and interpretation of meaning.

The point here is that we can hear something, but attending to and understanding its meaning, can be challenging.

With that said, there is no tool I know as effective at building a strong bond as listening. In our 'never can get enough ' interaction world, where we now twitter to each other every time we have even a synapse of a thought, we are losing the ability to be quiet and listen. I am known as a very outspoken and active therapist, meaning I have a lot to say and willing to say it. However, I think most people would be surprised to hear that what I consider my most important attribute is I LISTEN VERY CAREFULLY to everything my patients have to say. When they are talking I am listening closely.

Frequently, I will ask if they want input, and if they say no – I listen some more. Eventually, every adolescent I have known wants some feedback, and then I can begin. Prior to that, I just remain quiet and actively listen. By actively listening, I mean I feedback to the client much of what he is saying. I do this so we are both on the same page. He can see I am listening to each word, and he knows I understand his point of view. What this says to him is, "What you have to say is important, and I want to thoroughly understand it before we go any further".

Feeding statements back to adolescents allows them to clarify meaning. Often they are communicating emotionally, and hearing it from me allows them to re-think it and clarify where necessary.

Let's take a look at Mark. He was a 15 year-old boy who came to see me because his parents felt Mark was not communicating with them. The following is a brief interchange between us:

Mark: I hate my parents. They really suck. They never let me do what I want to do and it really pisses me off.

Dr. Matt: You hate your parents......?

Mark: OK, maybe not hate, but they really irritate me.

Dr. Matt: OK, so they may be good people, but they really irritate you a lot of times, especially when they don't let you do stuff.

Mark: Right

The change from 'hating' your parents to 'they are good people, but irritate me' is important for me to understand, and also for Mark to understand. This change was due to listening carefully, feeding back, and allowing Mark to clarify. Therefore, it is his idea that he does not 'hate' his parents, but just does not like some of their behavior – a much easier issue to resolve.

Now, listening and clarifying is extremely hard to do when it is your child, and they are going on and on about something. But believe me, they will notice you are not jumping in to quiet them, correct them, scold them, moralize to them, etc. You just want to understand them before doing or saying anything.

If they challenge you on why you are acting this way, just say it is important that you understand where they are coming from and that when they are done; hopefully, there will be time for you to chime in. Most adolescents will be taken totally off guard by this, as they usually see discussions as a time for arguing.

RESPECTING

This one can be very, very challenging, but here we go. Try to maintain respect for your child, EVEN WHEN THEY MAY BE DISRESPECTFUL TO YOU. Remember, you are a role model as well as a parent. Most teens become disrespectful when they are frustrated. When they do, you should either ask them what is frustrating them or take a break and say we can start back when we can respect one another. Remember, most talks with adolescents span days and even weeks. You are not going to run out of time to make your point.

Think about when people speak to you. I would bet my last dollar that you are far more likely to listen to someone who treats you with respect than someone whom you feel does not respect you. It is the same way with adolescents. This is one of the reasons I have so many kids who want to come to therapy. They know I respect them even when I disagree with them.

This should also be one of the foundational rules in all families. It is important that family members treat each other with respect. Granted there will be times when this does not happen, but the overall tone in any well functioning family is that the members have respect for one another.

BRIDGING STATEMENTS

This is a great tool, which is not used often enough. These statements are crucial with all people, but more so with adolescents. A bridging statement is a reaffirmation of how you feel about the adolescent, or an opportunity to ask how they feel about you. Let's look at an example from a discussion I had with a 17 year-old named Chuck.

Chuck: Doc, I have decided I am going to drop out of school at the end of the year.

Dr. Matt: And do what?

Chuck: I think I will just live on the road, hitching around and try to find jobs as I go.

Dr. Matt: Chuck, you know I care about you, right? (BRIDGE)

Chuck: Yeah.

Dr. Matt: So I feel compelled to tell you I think this is a dangerous idea.

Chuck: Why?

Dr. Matt: Because I think you're a smart kid (Bridge) and you have lots of skills (Bridge) you could develop by finishing high school. I just do not know anyone who has been successful who has dropped out of high school to "live on the road". You can always experiment with this after you graduate because at least then you will have a high school diploma. If you want to try it then – go for it, but for now I think you should finish high school. I respect that this is a tough decision (BRIDGE) so all I am asking is you consider what I am saying before doing anything radical. OK?

Chuck: I hate school, but I will think about what you said.

Dr. Matt: I know I am giving you feedback that does not agree with your point of view - are you OK with me being so upfront with you?

Chuck: Its cool. I would rather you are straight with me than blow smoke at me.

Dr. Matt: I am glad you feel this way. You know I respect you (BRIDGE) and part of that is I want to always be upfront with you.

Chuck: Chill.

    This series of bridges both confirms and affirms how I feel about Chuck, while allowing me to say things he does not want to hear and at which he might otherwise take offense. This is all set up by really listening to what Chuck had to say, letting him know I think he is smart and what he says has value, verbally telling him that I respect him, and placing my own opinion in the ring to be considered.

    This same conversation could have gone a very different way:

Chuck: Doc, I have decided I am going to drop out of school at the end of the year.

Dr. Knucklehead: What a stupid idea. Don't you know you can't do anything without a high school diploma?

Chuck: I don't care about that.

Dr. Knucklehead: Chuck, you are being very immature. You have no chance of succeeding.

Chuck: Screw you. I am going to do what I want.

Which of these two interchanges has the best probability of getting Chuck to consider finishing high school? I think it is easy to see that when you approach adolescents in a respectful, open manner you have a much better chance of being heard and considered.

LISTENING MOMENTS VS. TEACHING MOMENTS

This can get a little frustrating for parents, but the truth of the matter is that most moments are listening moments, not teaching moments. Parents are in a very powerful role where they can be a role model listening as well as using their role to get their adolescents to respect them. It is hard to get irritated at someone who is committed to listening to your position (no matter how ridiculous it may be).

I cannot tell you the number of times I have let adolescents say something nutty, and they have kept talking until they have talked themselves out of it. My favorite example of this was in a discussion with Cole, a 16 year-old with a crush on a girl in his class.

Cole: Dr. Matt, I heard Jackie is going to be at the pier with her friends on Saturday afternoon. I really want to ask her out but I am not sure how to do it.

Dr. Matt: (foolishly thinking it would be something sane) Well, what are you thinking about?

Cole: Well, I've been thinking about it and I think I have a cool plan. I think when I see her, she will be with all her friends – that would make it weird for me to go up to her and ask her out. So what I think

I will do is run down the pier naked and do a full dive into the surf in front of them.

Dr. Matt: (Lots and lots of stunned silence and a quizzical look) So your plan is to jump naked off the pier?

Cole: Yeah!!!

Dr. Matt: What if she sees you and does that first?

Cole: What are you talking about?

Dr. Matt: Well, a cool plan like that could go both ways. Maybe she will get naked and jump off the pier while you and your friends are watching. Wouldn't that be cool?

Cole: Are you serious? I would puke. That would be totally weird. I don't want my friends seeing her nude and thinking she's crazy.

Dr. Matt: (SILENCE) HMMMM.

Cole: (LOTS OF THINKING) You know maybe I better not do that — it would make me look kind of weird. What do you think?

Now remember this is all happening in real time. I could have said something about him looking nuts and that he might offend her, but it is much more powerful if he comes to that conclusion and tells me the plan needs changing (by the way, if he had not gotten to that insight I would have gone with plan B and talked to him directly. But again, his coming to this conclusion makes it a done deal in his own mind).

Too often parents believe situations are teaching moments when they are really listening moments. If an adolescent talks himself out of a silly situation he does two important things. First, his esteem will rise because he has thought of it. Second, he is much more likely to follow through on the better plan because it is his plan.

REVIEW

1. Listening – This can be your most powerful tool as a parent. Knowing how to really listen and allowing your adolescent to see you are really listening can go a long way to building and maintaining positive contact with your adolescent. Most adolescents will tell you all about themselves if you take the time not to interject and to hear what they are saying.

2. Respect – One of the major components of any positive relationship is respect. It may be difficult to show this at times but if you can maintain this level of understanding in your relationship, you are far more likely to have positive results. This does not mean agreeing with your adolescent but it does mean listening, taking turns in conversations, lecturing less and inquiring more, and not disparaging the character of your adolescent.

3. Bridging Statements – These are powerful tools for encouraging a conversation to continue while letting your adolescent know you feel positively about them as an individual, whether you agree or disagree with what he is saying. Use them frequently.

4. Listening Moments vs. Teaching Moments – Most of the moments you spend with your adolescent will be listening moments. However, every once in a while a teaching moment will present itself and you can use it to the max since you do this so infrequently. Most parents fall into the trap of believing that most moments are teaching moments, which make adolescents want to share less.

CHAPTER 2

THE THREE C'S - CREATE A CULTURE OF COMMUNICATION

Some things you can wait on, others you cannot – this one belongs to the latter group. The earlier you start to create a culture of communicating in your home, the more ingrained in your children it will be. Many families do not know how to speak to one another. They spend virtually no time developing this skill and therefore, do not have it in place when it is needed.

I have seen far too many situations where having a communication plan in place would have saved a lot of heartache. A painful example of this can be seen when an adolescent has made a mistake and hurt a parent's feelings. The parent then decides that he will not speak to the adolescent until the adolescent apologizes. This often leads to a prolonged period of non-communication (and in divorced families, where time is split and so seeing the offended parent is also disrupted, this can be a real disaster). While each situation is different, most of the time it is the parent's responsibility to approach the adolescent and help him to understand, not just the painful part of what happened, but how to heal it. Most adolescents box themselves into a corner and need the loving guidance of a parent (even a hurt parent) to help them out. Having the non-hurt parent help in these situations is also a huge plus. Waiting for your adolescent to approach you will almost always lead to a lot more pain.

Dr. Glenn at the University of Iowa published an interesting study. He looked at the amount of time parents spent interacting with their children in the 1950's and compared it to families in the 1980's. Before you read on, stop for a second and try to guess the answers to these questions. How much time do you think parents spent communicating with their children in the 50's? How about the 80's? Well let's look.

What Dr. Glenn found was that in the 1950's parents spent about 4 hours per day interacting with their children. It was a different time and families were much more dependent on each other. In addition, distractions from the computer age were not available. By the 1980's this 'family time' had dwindled to about 12 minutes per day. And when dissected further, 10 of the 12 minutes parents spent with their kids was in correcting them. Thus parents spent about 2 minutes per day talking to their kids. And this was even before the proliferation of computers.

Everything else seems to get in the way of just talking to one another. This study occurred when there were significantly fewer outside distractions. Today with cell phones, texting, facebook, myspace, twitter, mytwitbookspace, etc., it is a minor mIracle if people communicate to one another in person at all.

My belief is that now, more than any other time in our history, it is important to carve out a time and place for families to speak to one another about their lives. I will use a sports analogy here. When you see a player or team win a championship it is often inspiring. However, I always remind families that the moment they are watching is not when the championship was won. Championships are won late at night, in dimly lit gyms, with no one around but the players. They are won on the outside courts with years of practice and no cheering. They are won at 5 AM on snow-covered rinks by the teams who wake up and skate. These times did not seem important when they were occurring but they laid the groundwork for the ultimate victory. The same is true in communicating with your adolescent. All the silly, fun, seemingly unimportant talks lay the groundwork for when you really need to discuss something with your adolescent. Those seemingly unimportant 'practices' are just as important, as they set the stage for your championship talks.

So let's look at some options, which are still doable in today's world with today's adolescents:

1. **THE DINNER TABLE** – This is still a mainstay in the lives of most families. The dinner table is one of the best places to have family time together. Starting at a young age, dinner should be a priority in a home. You know those families who sit with a television blaring at the dinner table, and everyone's listening to it. In those families parents and children learn more, and know more, about their favorite television characters than they do about each other. Remember, there will come a day when all that prep time at the dinner table will pay off. You will actually have a forum to discuss more sensitive topics, which may affect the lives of your kids. When a big issue does come up, you are going to want a forum to discuss it. It will be useful if that forum does not include watching the television (which happens in more than 50% of households with children according to the Federal Trade Commission Survey). I doubt anyone wants television giving his or her children advice - then why invite TV to the table at all?

Dinner-time should be a time to talk about the day or bring up any issues that you or your kids would like to discuss. This often will be very pleasant conversation with kids sharing what went well today. I suggest parents start this early by talking to each other about their days. This provides a model for kids of what is expected at the dinner table as well as keeping the parental connection strong. And, by the way, we are not looking for perfection. This may happen only 4 days a week in your home, but 4 days is infinitely better than zero days.

2. **CAR TIME** - (See Dinner Table). Same movie - different theater. The car is a wonderful place to snare an adolescent and have time with him. Do not allow him to have headphones on in the car. Entertainment centers in cars, while good for some situations, take the air out of conversation. Use them wisely. As with dinner, you do not have to have a discussion each time you are in the car, but it is nice to know you can when the need arises.

3. **FAMILY MEETINGS** - These should occur about once a month and everyone should have the opportunity to be heard. These are not

gripe-fests, but time to actually discuss issues. Tell kids that they should have a tentative solution for each of the problems they are bringing up. It may not be the one we adopt, but it shows they have done more than just complain. Take notes; let the kids know this counts and change things when you can. Again, highlight why you are changing it and your kids will begin to see these times as opportunities to have a say in the home. In addition, with a meeting once a month, there is no harm in telling a child that you will try it their way for two weeks (or a month), and then reassess how it is working. If it is going well, the new idea will stay. If not, you can reassess.

4. **DOING SOMETHING WITH YOUR CHILD** - I have a basketball hoop at my office in the back parking lot. I shoot hoops with a number of kids who come see me. I have cards in my office and we will often play crazy eights while we talk. You would be surprised how much easier the conversation goes when we are both engaged in something fun. There is much less pressure, and the adolescent does not feel he is 'trapped' in the doctor's office. We are just two people, shooting hoops, playing cards, discussing what is happening. I used to watch my mother and father do this in various ways. It was really fun to be part of what they were doing, and it allowed us time to talk and laugh and just bond. Find those things in your home and use them to create a communication bond.

5. **SCHEDULING TIME WITH YOUR ADOLESCENT** – This is a great idea for a couple of reasons. Primarily, it gives you unfettered time with your child in a setting of your liking. It also says you respect your adolescent. Make sure to tell him that you see his time as valuable too. Scheduling a time gives you both an opportunity to have your get together at a convenient time.

6. **TELEVISIONS SHOULD NOT GO IN A CHILD'S BEDROOM** - This is one of the surest ways to make sure you never see your adolescent. Kids with televisions in their bedroom have a much easier time avoiding communication than those who do not (and approximately 64% of kids have a television in the bedroom). The latest survey on

television watching in children and adolescents finds that kids watch about 3 hours and 20 minutes of television per day, or about 23 hours per week. This is an entire day! Most adolescents are not a fountain of information at best. If you allow them to hibernate in their bedrooms, you may not see them for 6 or 7 years (which may send some parents out to buy a television for their adolescent today). If they want to watch television it should be in a family room where interactions are much more possible.

7. **COMPUTERS SHOULD NOT GO IN A CHILD'S BEDROOM** - See 'Televisions Should Not Go In a Child's Bedroom' and multiply it by ten. The computer should be used in a public place where parents can monitor what is going on. If it must go in a child's room (and there should be an incredibly good reason for this), then a parent should have full and open access to it at all times. Access to the Internet brings many positive experiences into your child's world, but many hazardous ones as well. It is up to you to police this avenue. In addition, adolescents should not have access to a social networking site unless the parent has the password to that site. When you have access to your child's facebook, etc., you have a clear view into his world. This is why I often suggest to parents to allow adolescents to have this kind of forum, as long as the parent is the monitor.

8. **COMPUTER GAMES** - I have seen many adolescents become addicted to computer games. It is not their fault. The games are addicting. However, I think there should be firm limits built in by parents around time of usage and what games are played. The idea that kids will make good decisions in the face of such an attractive alternative is silly. It is like sending your kid into a candy store and hoping he brings back broccoli. The temptation is just too high and your adolescent needs rules around engagement to help him negotiate this 'fun' part of his life. In addition, there is also the issue of detachment, which I see in my office quite a bit. This is when your child knows far more about the game characters he interacts with than about his friends, family, school, etc. Again, there is nothing

wrong with giving it your all, but it should be balanced with other 'real' parts of your life.

I have seen this singular focus firsthand. When I ran the adolescent inpatient drug unit, we experienced a short period where we were seeing little progress from our patients. We had a team meeting and were discussing why the group format seemed to be dragging. The interactions among the kids had become quite superficial and the allegiances between kids on the unit, which helped foster sobriety, were lacking. We did a behavioral assessment for a week and found that we were allowing far too much time for playing computer games. We had a computer system set up in the group room, and the adolescents were frantically using it. Usually this room was for kids to get together, talk among themselves, and build relationships and bond. We thought the game would help foster this. What we found was that the game gave them something to talk about OTHER THAN THEMSELVES and so relationships were not being formed. In fact the most powerful relationships appeared to be between the kids and the characters in the game. We quickly limited access and found that the kids seamlessly went back to building relationships and supporting one another.

REVIEW

1. One of the foundations of any strong family is their ability to communicate effectively with one another. Creating a Culture of Communication is one of the primary duties of any parent.

2. Communicating with your children creates a platform that is enjoyable and will be useful when an important discussion needs to be held. Those 'big' parent-child talks you have are built on all those little ones you have had over the years.

3. Communicating with your child should start very early in a child's life and be something that is a given in every family's routine.

4. I have listed 8 areas which you should examine and use to foster communication, i.e. dinner time, car time, family meetings, doing something with your child, scheduling time with your adolescent, televisions should not go in a child's bedroom, computers should not go in a bedroom, computer games. The first 5 should be encouraged, the next two should be avoided and the last one should be monitored.

CHAPTER 3

OPEN TOUGH SUBJECTS …..AND WAIT FOR THAT SILENCE

This is one of the more difficult behaviors for parents to adopt. They are often faced with whether to address a sensitive subject like drug usage, sex, etc., or whether to ignore it. When in doubt, I think you should ask. What asking does is open the door to a number of positive opportunities.

1. It tells your adolescent that you care enough to ask tough questions.

2. It tells them you think they are old enough to engage in this kind of conversation. In fact, I use this as a bridging statement (see Chapter 'Listen….And They Will Tell You Exactly Who They Are'). For instance a parent might say, "Prior to now, I was unsure as to whether or not you could talk to me intelligently about this. However, as you have grown, I see you as older and more mature so I want to know what are your thoughts on kids using drugs"?

3. It lets them know your head is not in the clouds and that you are really paying attention to them.

4. It lets them know you know what is going on in the world and possibly their peer group.

5. It opens the door for more conversation on the topic later.

6. It allows you to open other sensitive doors more easily.

7. It lets your child know you are not afraid of sensitive topics.

Often you will be met with silence or rejection. Take this as a good sign. It means that your adolescent heard what you said. If they had not heard you, you would not get this kind of response. It is very common for an adolescent to mull these questions over, and return with an answer in the near future. After all, you have probably caught them off guard and they need to think about it. It is often a good idea to let them know that they can think about it and get back to you. Discussions like these do not have a definitive beginning and end. They are open-ended and should progress as your adolescent grows.

The reason I strongly recommend parents discuss sensitive topics with their adolescents is that if you do not address these subjects; your adolescent will not bring them up. They do not know what kind of reaction they will get if they tell you they want to have sex, etc. And if they do not bring it up, they will be getting their information from friends, or worse – television and the Internet. Talk about influences you do not want teaching your adolescent!

In addition, do a little research before you speak. You will not be taken seriously if you do not have at least a little 'street cred' (if you do not know what this means consult your adolescent). For instance, your adolescent is not going to engage you in a discussion on drugs if you ask them if anyone has offered them a 'marijuana cigarette'. However, if you ask if anyone has tried to get them to 'blow dope' this immediately tells your adolescent you have some idea about drug usage.

Know some background around the subject you are talking about. If you are going to discuss a subject your kid knows something about, at least do enough research to allow you to engage them in a conversation about it. For instance, if you are talking about marijuana it might help to know that 4/20 is national smokeout day. It will probably surprise your adolescent you are aware of that. How about being able to discuss that 3-4 teens sitting in a car with rolled up windows to keep the smoke in, is called a hotbox (and one of the surest ways to have an officer stop to investigate what is going on). Anyway, knowing something about a subject will tell your kid, 'I am not out to lunch', 'I know a little about your world', and 'I am not afraid to discuss it'.

Now, I always have to add two modifiers to this advice. I have had some overzealous parents who hear this advice and cannot control themselves, so every time they see their adolescent they are asking about drugs, sex, etc. This is a gigantic turnoff to adolescents and will actually make them avoid you. Bringing up sensitive subjects should be used wisely and when needed. Adolescents are notoriously poor at covering their tracks. They are far too impulsive and unplanned thereby almost always erring in hiding things they do not want their parents to know. When a parent tells me they do not know if their adolescent is using drugs that almost always means their adolescent is NOT using drugs because it is very hard for an adolescent to keep this hidden. Therefore, you will know when it is time to have one of these discussions by listening and watching your adolescent.

The second modifier is to have these talks when things are going well, not during a fight, etc. Do you like to discuss sensitive material when you are fighting? Probably not. Take your adolescent for a ride or out to lunch. Let them know that you care about their world and want to know about it. Then you are setting the table for discussions, which should happen throughout your lives.

I know this lesson from personal experience. My mother and I have always been very close. We have had countless discussions regarding almost everything under the sun. I am now older and go back to my hometown of Buffalo frequently. Each time, my mom and I set some time aside to talk about anything and everything. Some of these talks focus on funny things, some on important things. Some of our discussions I think about months, and even years later. These heart-to-heart talks do not just happen; they have been going on since I was a kid. This is something I love and a gift which I hope I am able to share with my children.

REVIEW

1. There are at least 7 excellent reasons to discuss difficult subjects with your adolescent. Although this may seem challenging, the benefits far outweigh the awkwardness.

2. Frequently, I see parents who 'wish' their adolescent would speak to them about the difficult subjects they face in their teens, i.e., drugs, independence, sex, etc. Who do you think will be more comfortable bringing up these subjects (I will give you a hint – it is not your adolescent)?

3. Let your adolescent know you believe he can handle this more adult-like conversation and you want it to be part of your relationship.

4. When you are rebuffed (and most of the time you will be), your adolescent will hear you are open to these subjects. This may not be important at the moment, but at some point he will be happy to have you in his corner when he is faced with a difficult decision.

5. The two things to keep in mind here are to use these opportunities to discuss sensitive topics wisely (do not overuse it), and bring these topics up when your relationship is going well, not during a fight.

CHAPTER 4

UNDERSTAND, EMPATHIZE AND ABOVE ALL DISCIPLINE

These three words seem to get muddled in the vocabulary of most parents – understanding, empathizing, and disciplining. The reason for this is kids do a great job of confusing parents by arguing their point. After a while kids convince parents that "they simply don't understand" when the parent is disciplining. "Weren't you kids once" or "You just don't understand" are common adolescent refrains. Parents often buy into these arguments, giving kids weapons to use later on. It is important to keep the definitions of these words clear to yourself, whether or not your child agrees.

Let's take an easy example. I understand why OJ 'allegedly' killed his wife – he was jealous. I get it and so does probably every person who has ever been jealous in his or her life. However, understanding does not mean I condone it, and it surely does not mean it is OK. It never means it should go unpunished. A parent can completely understand their child's behavior, and even his motives, but that does not excuse behavior in any way. Do you understand why people take drugs? Of course you do – momentarily they feel better. Would you allow your adolescent to do this because you understand this?

I can also understand empathizing with kids. Wouldn't you like to egg someone who was not nice to you? Of course you would. However, you do not because it is wrong and not the way to handle the situation. Aren't there things in a store which you would love to have, but just cannot afford right now? I can empathize with that, but it is still not OK to steal them.

Kids need to be disciplined exactly because you CAN understand and even empathize with them. This is most important to explain to your adolescent. Much of their behavior is easily understandable, but it is wrong and needs to be curbed.

Thus, the tactic to take with kids is to agree that you understand and tell them why. Agree that you empathize and can even relate to their behavior. AND with that said, the discipline continues.

BUT IT'S NOT FAIR

Kids LOVE to use "But it's not fair". It is such a pithy bomb to drop when needed. They really want you to buy into this. When you attempt to be fair all the time you are placing yourself in a very vulnerable position as well as not doing a good job of teaching your child about the realities of the world.

The difficulty many parents have is that they are afraid of being seen as unfair, or possibly being unfair at times. Many parents want their children to view them as always being fair and overseeing everything. If you get to that point, let me know because I have yet to meet that Being. Therefore "but it's not fair" should be met with a solid "That may be" and then we will still do it this way.

I will give an example from my days as the Clinical Director of an inpatient drug unit for adolescents. There were many tough adolescents on this unit and one evening something happened with a nurse that the adolescents felt was unfair. They called a meeting the next day with me after I had been briefed (by the way, I think they had a valid point which at least called into question what happened).

Dr. Matt: Hi everyone. I am here at your request. Is there one of you who is the spokesperson for you guys?

Josh: Me, Josh.

Dr. Matt: Great. Go ahead Josh. Let me know what is up.

Josh: What happened last night was really unfair and we don't like the s#$@t that went down.

Dr. Matt: OK. You're probably right.

LONG SILENCE

Josh: Well, what are you going to do about it?

Dr. Matt: I am not going to do anything about it; although you may have a point that what happened was unfair.

LONGER SILENCE

Dr. Matt: It is hard for me to tell what actually happened and in such a case I will side with my staff. Therefore you may be correct and yet I will stand by the discipline and adhere to it.

Josh: But that's not fair.

Dr. Matt: You all know me and I try to be fair when I can. However, when it is not possible to tell what is really fair, I will side with the staff — which means at times you might not be treated fairly. Therefore, understand that many things that happen here, like in life, may not always be fair.

SILENCE

Dr. Matt: Do you guys have anything else for me or can we adjourn and get on with our lives?

Believe it or not that ended the meeting and I never heard about this again. Why? Because I had agreed that it might have been unfair (I did not need them telling me all the reasons). However, they could see I WAS NOT AFRAID OF BEING UNFAIR - that was not the issue. The issue was that the staff was in charge. I was not there when the incident occurred and, therefore, could not make an accurate assessment. I attempt to be fair when I can, and I have treated them with respect. Although I can try to help them understand and accept that situations are sometimes unfair, they ultimately will have to deal with the unfairness. And by the way, as I said, my goal is not to make everything fair. In fact, there may be other unfair situations that happen in their lives. I hope they learn to deal with those as well.

SUPPORT IS MORE IMPORTANT THAN FAIRNESS

It was more important for me to support my staff than dig into this. This is the same with parenting. I am amazed at how often parents fight about unfairness to a child instead of saying, "It may be unfair, but I side with your mom anyway". If a parent disagrees, that is a discussion for behind closed doors, not in front of your child. The last thing you want to teach your child is that if they yell "UNFAIR" you will jump into an investigative mode. If you do, you will be starting down a path, which leads to constant review and an increased probability of conflict with your spouse. The only exception to this rule is if a child is being abused. Then, of course, the non-abusing parent must take control and stop this behavior. Thankfully, this is the case in a very small percentage of situations.

PRACTICALITY TRUMPS THEORY

When in doubt, always choose practicality. Often times I will get parents who want their adolescent to act a certain way 'because that's how it's supposed to be'. In their head, they have a theory regarding the way things should go and it is not working. So what do they do? They apply the theory even more stringently, which, not surprisingly, also does not work.

I see this often when I suggest that parents reward adolescents for their grades. "Why should I? It's what they are supposed to do", I will hear. The answer is incredibly easy - "Because it works"!

I ask parents a simple question. Let's say your child is psychiatrically ill. I have two ways to treat the child. One is a theoretical model with a 50/50 chance of working. The other is, I dress as a clown and paint my face blue, which will work 100% of the time, but has no theory behind it. Which would you choose?

We see this in the media when a staunch right wing person has a child who is gay. They are now faced with embracing their theory or the reality that they love their child. I have rarely seen anyone choose theory over practicality in this case.

Theories are great, but what is happening right in front of you with your own child should guide your behavior.

I NEED MY KID TO AGREE WITH ME

As your kids change developmental levels, they will obviously become much better at crafting reasons for their behaviors and misbehaviors. In addition, they will have strong rationales regarding why discipline is unnecessary. I do not discount their arguments since in rare exceptions they will bring up something that has not been considered. However, an Achilles heel of many parents, and one of the major reasons they do not discipline consistently, is that they want their adolescent to AGREE with the discipline.

I do not know about you, but if my boss said it was up to me whether to take a pay cut or just keep things the way they were, I would probably choose the latter. This is the same situation you are creating by asking your adolescent to condone their punishment. Can you believe they are not going to agree with you? That is to be expected and should have little to no effect on the discipline. I expect your insight and judgment to trump your adolescent's. You know when they need to be disciplined whether they agree or not (and on occasion the unthinkable will happen and they will agree).

COMMITMENT TO SELF

Many years ago I had a 17 year-old come and see me. His name was Joe. His parents were concerned because they thought he was immature and had trouble following rules that made the entire family run more smoothly (this is par for the course in adolescence). I used to get a kick out of the number of 'fantabulous' excuses he would create to get out of consequences. One particular rule he liked to break was bringing the car home on time.

I liked Joe and it was not hard to get him to agree that if he brought the car home by 9 PM each night, his parents would allow him to use it tomorrow. If he were later, he would lose it for two weeks. Joe thought this was great as it gave him the power over when he would get the car. We agreed we would accept no excuses.

A few weeks later his parents came rushing in telling me they had an 'emergency'. With Joe in the room they related that he had been driving down the freeway following his girlfriend's car. Suddenly, she had a blowout and coasted to the side of the road. Joe DECIDED to stop. They called for help from a call box, got the car towed to a gas station, and then he gave her a lift home..........at 9:45 PM. The girl's parents called Joe's parents to thank them for having such a wonderful and responsible son (which he showed here).

I looked at the parents and asked, "So what is the emergency? Your son made some important, mature decisions. This should be a cause for celebration". "Well, we said he would lose the car for two weeks if he was past 9 PM". I said "Yes, and......". "Well, he was past 9 PM," said the parents. "Exactly", I said. "But it was a good thing he did" said Mom and Dad. "Yes, and......" I said. Finally, I turned to Joe. "Joe" I said "You made a promise that you would get the car home by 9. Although you said it to your parents, you made that commitment to yourself. You put your word on the line and the consequences that follow". He agreed. "What do you think should happen" I asked. He said "I am going to be without the car for two weeks". "That's right" I said "and you should be extremely proud of yourself for making such a difficult and courageous decision. I mean you DECIDED to lose your ride for two weeks to support your girlfriend. You should wear this consequence as a badge of honor and have your girlfriend drive you around. Also have her brag to her friends that you made this decision on her behalf. I wonder how many boyfriends would have stood so strong for their girlfriend."

Then turning to the parents. "Many good decisions come with negative consequences that we must learn to deal with. Not all good decisions are met with balloons and cake. That does not invalidate the decision. In fact, it appreciates the decision. You should be doubly proud of your son. But that does not change his commitment. You invalidate him by letting him off the hook, when you should be supporting his words AND his decisions".

Over the next couple of weeks Joe's girlfriend drove him around and frequently told the story of what Joe had given up for her. She was proud of him and wanted people to know it. In addition, his parents gave Joe a number of perks reserved for older, more mature people because he had shown that he was able to make an older and more mature decision in the face of a consequence he did not like. Thus, Joe made out quite well while also being able to honor his commitment.

Joe became a police officer in our City. I still see him from time to time when he drives by my office. He often harkens back to this session as a real turning point for him and one of which he is still proud. He made a good call in the face of a consequence he did not want. I cannot think of a better description of personal strength and maturity. He had given his word and he would stand by it because it was HIS word. If his parents had let him off the hook, it would have invalidated the importance of standing behind your word and your commitments. Bravo to both Joe and his parents. He became a stronger man that day.

NO NEED TO ARGUE WITH KIDS

I am amazed at how parents talk and talk and talk to kids like they need their adolescent's permission before they can act. Again, the politically correct crowd has convinced many parents that it is damaging to a child's ego and self-esteem to not explain things. Blarney. All this does is set up a system where the child then expects the parents to be able to back up everything they decide. Remember, discussions are like playing a home game for a child. Suddenly, from having no chance to argue, there lays the possibility to manipulate one's parents. Is it any wonder that kids want to bait their parents into endless discussions? Notice how your adolescent never needs to discuss why they CAN go to a party, only why they CAN'T.

John Rosemond wrote a very insightful article titled "Parents Don't Have To Argue with Children". In it he implores parents to stop giving kids the opportunity to argue. Statements such as 'Because I am the parent' and 'I said so' are very effective. This does two things. First, it establishes the pecking order in the family which should always be parents first. Second, it tells a kid that sometimes the only answer is 'I say so'. Get used to it because I am the parent. This is much more empowering and also it lets the child know the place is safe, someone is in control who will not be manipulated, and when a parent says something he means it.

How many of you have kids who like to argue? I will tell you a little secret. No kid likes to argue. You have trained them to do so by your behavior (I will discuss this principle further in chapter 4 of the Traps section, titled 'The Kid's Dictionary'). It's funny; I do not remember any kids I grew up with being argumentative. Why, because the parents in our neighborhood would not argue. It was chores here, dinner here and bedtime now. That is all. Breaking of the rules led to negative consequences but again no discussion of why (we knew why).

Feel free to agree with your kid's feelings. I heard you or I can see why you feel this way is great. But do not try to get them to agree. This is just a waste of your time and an invitation to argue.

REVIEW

1. *Understanding* your adolescent, *empathizing* with your adolescent, and *disciplining* your adolescent are all different states of mind which should lead to different behaviors.

2. Adolescents are especially adept at muddying these waters by using such phrases as 'it's not fair'. It is a parent's responsibility to see through those muddied waters to the need to discipline when necessary.

3. Under most circumstances (with the exception of abuse), it is far more important for parents to support one another than to worry about being fair to their children.

4. When you agree to a contract with your adolescent, remember that it is not just about the contract, but also about honoring the adolescents' commitment to themselves. Therefore excuses and reasons for violation of the contract should be understood (and sometimes even applauded), but not change the contract.

5. When faced with a decision between doing something on principle, which may work, and doing something practical, which will work, choose the latter.

6. Parents often carry their own baggage in terms of their own misconceptions (such as 'I must always be fair', or 'I need to adhere to my theoretical principles instead of doing what I know I should do', or 'I need my kid to agree with me'). These misconceptions warp the judgment of parents which is all an adolescent needs to bypass appropriate consequences.

7. The traps adolescents set, and we sometimes set for ourselves, skew parental behavior resulting in adolescents believing the world will function in this manner. Please do not create this disservice for your adolescent or the time they will learn this lesson will be under the consequences of a much less benevolent authority.

8. Arguing with your child is entirely under your control. Blaming a child for arguing is like blaming a horn for sounding. It is your job to discourage this behavior by not engaging your child in discussions around topics they have no say over.

CHAPTER 5

MAKE ADOLESCENTS RESPONSIBLE FOR THEIR OWN BEHAVIOR

Contracts with adolescents are usually quite effective if you keep one rule in mind. *Your adolescent needs you far more than you need your adolescent*. When was the last time your adolescent brought home dinner for the family, bought a house where you all could live, or took everyone out to the movies in the new car he bought for the family?

Far too many parents are conned into thinking their job is to give, give, give and when they are through with that to give a little more. It is not. Too often parents afford their children opportunities at a huge expense to themselves.

Along with this, too many parents take responsibility for their child's behavior. This robs the child of the necessary experiences that arise from the consequences of good and poor decisions. These learning moments are essential to help the adolescent learn to make good decisions. It is far better to experience these consequences when your child is younger and the consequences are minimal. As we get older, the consequences of our decisions are much greater and therefore can be much more costly.

As I stated in an earlier chapter, most house rules should be negotiable. Only those rules where the parent cannot tolerate error have to be set in stone. Therefore you want to teach your adolescent to be able to appropriately barter for what they want, and earn what they want from control of their own behavior.

I am often asked what works for a reward or consequence. For little kids it is easy to come up with things, i.e., candy, time playing games, extra time at night, etc. These can be given out for positive decisions. The child is allowed to pick one at a time or in a grab bag fashion (where the bag is filled with different rewards and the child can either look through them all and pick one or can just stick his hand in and grab one).

As kids get older, most of these rewards become less effective. Older kids are more discriminating. They like things that are often too expensive to use as a daily reward. Freedoms and choices tend to dominate their desires. It is during this time that parents need to get creative and use things that the adolescent receives everyday as a reward or punisher. This is where pendulum rewards and consequences come in handy.

PENDULUM REWARDS AND CONSEQUENCES

One of the best things to introduce to your teen is the concept of Pendulum Rewards & Consequences. A Pendulum Reward is a reward the child either earns or loses with regularity depending on their own behavior. Your job is not to judge the decision, but to be a scorekeeper and apply the reward or consequence as warranted. This is much easier said than done since many parents do not want to apply the consequences, even when their adolescents earns them. Prior to every contract, I warn parents of one thing – say what you mean and mean what you say. There are few actions worse than saying something and not following through because then your adolescent will accurately assume you do not mean what you say.

Let's look at an example - using the car. A good idea is to allow your child access to the car each and every day depending on his behavior with the car the day before. If your child brings the car home by 8 PM, he gets to use it the next day. If he is within 15 minutes, he loses it one day. If he is 30 minutes late, he loses it for 2 days. If he is over thirty minutes late, he loses it for one week, and if he is over 1 hour late, he loses it for two weeks. Therefore, it is really not up to you if your child gets the car, it is up to him. As I say to all my adolescents who lose something on the pendulum, I hope the extra 15 minutes was worth a day in your car because that was the cost. Good luck with your next decision.

Let's look at another common adolescent theme – the fight over curfew. Most adolescents want later curfews and most adults want earlier (although I would totally understand if adults just wanted their kids out of their hair). What you can do here is put your adolescent in full control of his own curfew. Let's say you want your child home at 9:30 and he wants 11. Now, assuming that there isn't anything really magical about 9:30 or 11, you can put your son or daughter in full charge. You do this by explaining that as a parent you really want 9:30 but you can understand wanting 11. What 99% of parents really want is for their child to act responsibly, do what they say, stay out of trouble and be responsible for their own time. This being the goal is exactly what you use to shape the curfew.

Tell the adolescent that the curfew is 9:30 for the next two weeks. If they are able to comply, and not be late, and show true responsibility around the time (this does not mean calling at 9:29 to say they are half an hour away), then the curfew will be 10:00 PM on day 15. Furthermore, if they follow through for the following two weeks, the curfew will change to 10:30 PM. Finally, if they follow 10:30 for the next two weeks, the curfew will jump to 11 PM and will stay at 11 PM until they blow it when it will revert to 10:30 PM (of course if they blow it at 10:30 PM, it goes back to 10 PM for two weeks, etc.). In this way the adolescent is always in charge of his curfew. When we do this in my office, I tell him I do not expect him to ever complain about curfew again because he is the one in charge and my response will be '"You have created your own problem and you have all the tools to fix it". Please do not complain to me. Also I let him know his parents are allowing him this control and that the parents are making no decision around curfew – the only decision being made is by the adolescent that is directly affecting his curfew.

Another question I frequently hear is whether parents should leave a 17 or 18 year-old alone for a weekend. If there is a strong reason not to do this (for instance, he just got out of rehab or has a history of negative behavior when left alone), the answer is an easy no. But again, most adolescents are nice people and parents want to know how they can assure themselves nothing will happen. My suggestion is that they speak with their adolescent and let him know this is a trial run. If things go well, there will be more opportunities for independence in the near future. If things do not go well, then being left alone will be off the table for 6 months. Again, it is the adolescent's behavior that will dictate the amount of freedom.

Lastly, with the advent of technology has come the cell phone. I do not know a single adolescent who does not want one. Parents on the other are incredulous when they call the phone and the adolescent does not answer. My input is that the phone comes with one rule – when a parent calls, it is always answered. If this does not happen, it costs the adolescent a week without the phone. So if "The battery is dead", it costs a week. If '"I left it in the car", it costs you a week, etc. There is simply no excuse. You can also specify different rules for different hours of the day. You are allowed not to answer between the hours of 7AM – 8 PM, other than that we expect you to answer or pay the price. I will be discussing fun in the next chapter, but an example here is appropriate. Instead of taking away the phone for not answering it, explain that anytime you call after 8PM and do not get a reply, you will simply drive over to your adolescent's girlfriend's home just to make sure things are OK. I assure you that phone will be answered at any cost.

Most adolescents leap at the chance to control their own destinies. When they err I suggest that parents neither lecture nor scold. A decision has been made and a consequence has occurred..........welcome to the real world. If your adolescent complains, it is OK to commiserate. Sometimes you cannot tell how costly the price is until you experience it yourself. Again, this is important to learn early when the cost is low.

With more escalated behaviors, decisions can take on very serious consequences. For instance, a drug abuser in the home is told that when he comes home high, he will be grounded for one month. If he does it again, it will be three months. If it happens a third time, he is either in rehab or a structured boarding school or out on the street (assuming he is 18). As I say to all young people, I do not have time to worry about whether you are using drugs. I cannot follow you around and would not even if I could. That is your decision. Just do not complain to me when you experience the consequences of your decision. The decision to use drugs was yours and yours alone. The price of using has been set and you will need to know it when calculating what you will do. Complaining after you have bought the punishment is just a waste of my time. Stand proudly and say you chose it and now have it.

I tell adolescents that the decision and price are pre-set. I know if I go to a car dealership and want to buy a car, I will have to pay. In the same way, if an adolescent is at a party and wants to stay out after curfew, the price is set. There may be times that it is worth the price, then do it and be proud you did it. The only behavior I will not accept is whining about the price when it has to be paid. If that occurs, we need to treat the adolescent more like a child and impose rewards and consequences until they are mature enough to accept responsibility for their decisions.

You will notice this takes all the air out of excuses, e.g., I could not get a ride home, I lost my cell phone, etc. A boundary has been violated with a preset price. If your child is late for curfew because he saved a baby from a burning home, he should be applauded and appreciated and rewarded in some way – his curfew also moves back one half hour.

Two caveats are important here. First, notice how the pendulum does not have a death penalty. Your child can get back on the horse after they experience the pain of their decisions. Second, this is all about decision-making. As I say to kids, if it is worth you losing your car for a week to stay that extra half hour with your girlfriend, then be proud of your decision. Do not try to weasel out of the cost. Your behavior says it was worth it. Maybe there will be times when the price is worth the consequence – then go for it.

This kind of thing takes parents out of the process of having to discipline; the discipline is COMPLETELY the responsibility of the adolescent. I tell parents they can SILENTLY root for one behavior over another, but they are just a scorekeeper here. It is the decisions of the adolescent, which will dictate exactly how long he can stay out, if he can use the car, etc. Most adolescents love this since they want more responsibility. What we are doing is teaching them a system for managing themselves while building in safety nets for parents.

ORGANIZE – DONT MORALIZE

This is a tough one since most parents want their adolescent to act more like adults. They are not – they are human. They try a lot of things and most do not work. This means they are often disorganized - not just their behavior but their thinking as well.

Telling your kid they SHOULD do something like clean the dog poop, etc., is only going to lead to frustration for you and your adolescent. Rather, create an environment where picking up the dog poop is part of the environment.

If your child cleans the poop something good happens. If not, they lose something. Let them know this is how life works. If I go to work and do well I not only feel good, I get paid – in money, cars, homes, etc. If I do not, I may still feel OK, but I lose all the perks.

Keep a large visual board in the house where rules are listed, including stuff they do (homework) and stuff you do (cook, clean, rides to events, etc.). Engage your adolescent in being organized. After all, it is not the event which is important; it is the process of being organized that makes the difference.

This understanding is a great gift that keeps giving all through life. Look at social drift data and recognize that people who are disorganized usually do not do well in life. How many of these people would be much better off if they could just organize themselves?

If adolescents came with a manual, let me tell you - they would not have read it. When that little baby is lying in your arms, the hospital should slap a patch on him/her, which reads, "Someday this adorable little baby is going to do some very foolish things – be prepared".

Again a caveat. No kid is perfect, no kid is even close. I give them some areas they can keep messy. I do not work on kids' rooms. Does it really matter if a kid keeps a messy room? This is your child's area. If he wants to live like a slob, close the door (this does not include leaving food in the room which causes bug infestation and house damage).

You are not moralizing; you are organizing when you have these templates in your home. It is much like losing weight – it happens in homes, which are organized around healthy eating, not homes which just speak about it.

REVIEW

1. The adolescent war cry is 'Give me control of my own life'. By making adolescents responsible for their own behaviors we not only give them control over much of what they do, but they also get control over how tightly they are restricted.

2. Remember your adolescent needs you more than you need your adolescent.

3. Pendulum rewards and consequences are very effective in helping parents to remove themselves from adolescent angst. The parent's job is to create the criteria whereby an adolescent can achieve some of his goals depending on his behavior. Along with that perk come consequences for less healthy behavior. The parent then is transformed into an interested bystander and scorekeeper, and the adolescent has no one to blame or applaud for his current circumstances but himself.

4. Pendulum rewards and consequences can be applied to a large class of behaviors. Once kids are taught how this works, they can often create ways to implement it that help them and their parents.

5. In addition, when you use rewards and consequences in this manner, it eliminates the need to moralize. When you help your adolescent to organize, you have not only solved today's problem, but also provided your adolescent with a template for life.

CHAPTER 6

<u>HAVE FUN</u>

This is one of the most important lessons of parenting, and life – ENJOY YOUR KIDS. Before you know it, they will be gone.

In the chapter 'The 3 C's - Create A Culture of Communication', I mentioned a study by Dr. Glenn examining time spent communicating within families. Imagine only spending two minutes per day speaking with your child from birth to 18. That would amount to 13,140 minutes or a little more than the number of minutes in 9 days. Do you really want to spend that little time with your child? I doubt it. However, it appears that in many families, 2 minutes per day is a generous approximation.

One of the most hilarious parts of my job is clowning around with kids. For instance, when I get a resistant adolescent in my office, I often start the first session by saying something like "Well you're finally here – I heard you have been begging your parents to come and see me...take me to Dr Matt, take me to Dr. Matt, that's all I want - take me to Dr. Matt – today must feel like Christmas to you". This always gets a smirk, as the adolescent knows I am onto their stuff and willing to have some fun with it.

As I get to know an adolescent, one of my favorite approaches in working is to use humor. For instance, when I give homework I tell them there is a cost to not doing the homework. Almost inevitably they ask what can I do about it? About the homework nothing, but I can show up at your school, stand in the hallway and yell your name as I run up and down the hallway. God forbid I see you, as I may feel compelled to run up to you and give you a big bear hug – that would be fun wouldn't it? Again, although they know this would not happen they almost always laugh at the thought.

Parents can do these kinds of things too. When your kid does weird stuff (which they all do), I suggest you just follow right along.

If your kid has green hair and is prancing around when you have friends over, wait until his friends are over, put on a big green wig, the big glasses you bought at the 99 cent store, and jump right into their conversation. That gets a kid's attention real, real quick.

This is one of the reasons I always suggest to adolescents that they invite me to their parties. They always laugh when I say my invitation obviously got lost in the mail. "Where should I meet you and your friends?" or "Hey do you want me to come along on your date tonight – it will be really fun having your friendly neighborhood psychologist along" are always met with a laugh.

There is a deeper reason though, to use humor and laughing. The adolescent in your home is not just a problem. He is much more than that and most of this 'other stuff' is good. Sometimes adolescents begin to define themselves by their problems, e.g., "I am a bad kid", "I am a troublemaker", etc. These always have negative connotations. What is worse is that the entire communication pattern becomes focused on what is wrong and bad. It is hard to make changes when you are always discussing negative behaviors.

By way of example, one of the problems I see in our field is that sometimes people go to therapists because they have been physically or sexually abused. The therapy then focuses 100% on this issue and these circumstances *at the expense of all the rest of the person.* What this does is encourage the person to see himself only as a function of this incident rather than as a whole fully functioning multi-faceted person to whom something bad happened. The latter description allows for much more growth. The idea that you are all about one problem is stagnant and just replays the situation over and over. This is why although I will tell people they are abuse survivors, I make sure to tell them this is a badge of honor to be proud of; however, it is just one facet of who they are as a person. This does not fully define them; it is just part of who they are.

I see this same kind of narrow defining in high achievers as well. It drives me nuts when I hear someone say "I am a 3.8". I always say, "You are not a 3.8. Your name is Marie and you have many wonderful qualities. You have done well in school and you have earned a 3.8. Congratulations, but that is not you and never will be."

Let me tell you a story of a 13 year-old I saw when I worked at USC Medical Center (I'll call him 'Rick'). His mother had brought him to see me complaining that he never really spoke to her, didn't listen to her, and she feared she had lost touch with him. During our session it was apparent that he enjoyed talking about some topics, like sports, his friends, games, and so forth; but shied away from others, such as chores, school, etc. (funny how so many kids shy away from these topics). When I watched Mom and Rick, it was apparent that they really did want to communicate with each other, but just could not find a way.

One day I suggested we have our session out on the basketball court. Mom told me "No way", but Rick really wanted to. We struck a compromise where I would play with Rick, and Mom would stand on the sidelines and we would all talk throughout. This was fine until Rick and I devised a plan to get Mom involved. Every once in a while the ball would 'accidentally' roll over toward Mom. We would ask her to pick it up and throw it back. With a little encouragement she began to throw it at the basket (she was no Michael Jordan but she was trying). Anyway, before long, she and Rick were throwing the ball and shooting and laughing (I was seeing bench time). When the hour was up, we all walked toward my office. As we started toward the building, Rick's mom said, "Dr. Duggan, I would like to see you for a moment in your office, privately." I thought, "Uh-oh. Mom is upset because she did not want to play and we got her involved." When she sat down in my office she had only one thing to ask – "Do you know where I can buy a basketball and basket?" She told me she had not had that much fun with Rick since he was two or three. She did not realize she could enjoy doing things like that with him. She felt accepted by him and loved it.

As she left with the address of a sports store in her hand, I thought how silly I must have sounded out there, chiming in with what I thought were insightful comments. Mom and Rick could not have cared less. They were building a communication bridge with fun as the medium. Rick could see his mom in a different light other than someone who kept reminding him of his deficiencies (homework, chores, etc.) At the same time, he could show-off to her by doing something he was proud of, while also teaching her about something she did not know. Likewise, Mom had the courage to delve into a world (sports) where she did not feel confident and adopt the role of learner.

While that session did not totally change the situation, it went a long way to helping Rick and Mom learn to like, respect, and communicate with one another. We used that session as a touchstone in the weeks ahead. Not surprisingly, as the fun returned to Rick and Mom's relationship, verbal communication, mutual learning and the ability to solve problems returned as well.

Therapy not only can be fun, sometimes it is essential if people are going to learn to enjoy one another and re-establish a positive relationship.

As an aside, during a talk I gave to a group of professionals regarding this, a therapist raised his hand to ask me a question. He wanted to know if I had any ways to increase the 'fun quotient' during therapy sessions. HUH? I think he and I misunderstood each other. This isn't about quotients or formulas; it's about enjoying the person in front of you and establishing a relationship with fun as one of the foundations and solutions.

Fun is one of the basic building blocks of a good relationship. Just look at all your relationships that matter. I doubt you have any profound, important relationships that do not have fun as a building block. We trust those with whom we can laugh.

Lastly, if you can learn to laugh at your issues, instead of stew in them, you have gained an important skill that you can use anytime. Being able to laugh at a problem, minimizes it and places it in a context, which is much less scary. It also tells you that this is manageable.

A 19 year-old named Jim came to see me. He had a severe anxiety problem and would obsess on ideas which frightened him. Although he was a good looking young man and had plenty of sexual encounters with females, he would plague himself with thoughts that he must be gay. Now, I have no problem if someone is gay, but it was clear that Jim was not. He was picking an attribute, which he knew could not be 'proven', and pouring his internal anxiety into it. We spoke often of this process. Jim agreed that none of his behavior supported his belief (he had a girlfriend named Jane whom he liked) and most of his thoughts and behaviors directly contradicted homosexual tendencies (he had no longing for male attention, etc.). In fact, Jim himself announced, "I know this is not true, but the thought just keeps bugging me". We did a lot of cognitive behavioral work, where we examined the validity of Jim's thoughts, and Jim also went on a small dose of an anti-anxiety medication. Jim became much happier and actually was able to acknowledge that sometimes his internal anxiety made him come up with off the wall ideas on which to obsess. I knew we were almost at the end of therapy when we had the following conversation:

Dr. Matt: Jim, you seem a little down today.

Jim: I am

Dr. Matt: Are you feeling anxious today?

Jim: No, but I am thinking of calling it quits with Jane.

Dr. Matt: Why are you guys calling it quits?

Jim: (Delay) Cause I'm gay, don't you remember?

He had a huge smile on his face and was laughing. He was able to poke fun at his anxiety and his old obsessions. It was clear they did not have a grasp on him anymore.

NICKNAMES

These, like frames, are incredibly powerful tools used to shape behavior. In fact, I debated whether to place this section in the framing chapter, but decided to place it here because of the joy and fun nicknames can bring to a person.

I bet you have had a few nicknames throughout your life. I bet you could accurately tell me which ones were positive and which ones were not. Nicknames are not just names given to us, but ones we have EARNED. Therefore, I strongly encourage people to give nicknames to their children, ALWAYS POSITIVE ONES. Living up to nicknames will often guide actions.

Nicknames make us special. They highlight something about us, which is unique to us. It's very cool to have a nickname. It should be positive and highlight something you are proud of. Unlike frames, which can be either good or bad, we want to employ this tool only for the good. Therefore, we do not give nicknames like killer, bad boy, etc. The reason is obvious. This works as a template upon which we make decisions. Most of us want to live up to our nicknames since we have earned them, and we want others to keep using them. Telling someone they are a killer only increases the likelihood that they will act aggressively in situations where they are not sure what to do.

When I was a camp counselor, one of the first things I did was make sure everyone had a positive nickname - something that made them special in the group. If I had a child who was uncoordinated and was clearly the weakest link in the group, I might announce he was "Clipboard Man". I placed him in charge of the clipboard where all vital group information was kept so if you wanted to be rewarded at the end of the day, you had to make sure you treated Clipboard Man with respect. It is amazing how important this can become to a child and how proud they become of these names. It was not uncommon for parents to call me and let me know that for the first time in a child's life, the child was proud of himself and felt he had a niche, something that made him important in the group.

That's why I love to give kids nicknames and I tell them why. I had a young girl in my practice that had gone through some very severe experiences. She was continuing to get through school and was still on her volleyball team. She would not succumb to self-pity. My nickname for her was "The Rock". She knew she could cry, she knew she could be sad, but in the end she was going to achieve. I was proud of her.

I had another girl who was depressed over watching her best friend die. I suggested this was horrible, but also she had more experience in this than anyone else her age. Perhaps she could help others going through crises because of her vast pain and experience. Her nickname? "The Counselor".

I had another boy who got cut from his baseball team. We talked about going out next year. His nickname was "The Train" – he would not be slowed down.

One of my favorites is to label a kid a "Warrior". Think of how powerful that is to have someone you respect tell you, you are an inspiration and a warrior. Do you think that kid is going to give up when times get tough? Hell No! And not only that, he is going to tell you he did not give up because "I am a Warrior".

The power of telling a kid you can do it, and here is the name which describes you, is immense. I will actually have this talk with kids as they come to see me. They love picking out a name, which describes their best behavior. When they are focused on their best behavior, it is hard to have time to screw up.

I had one of my adolescents tell me that he stopped smoking dope because he saw himself as an athlete, and serious athletes do not smoke dope. Not coincidentally his nickname was 'The Athlete'.

In the same vein, I have had many students who have not done well in school come to therapy, like it, and want to enter the field. I tell them they must do better in school, and I nickname them 'Doc'. It is amazing to see how hard most of them work to keep this title. They see themselves differently with this nickname, and it significantly affects their behavior.

One caveat here, is you may run into an adolescent who has an especially good sense of humor and can poke fun at himself with a nickname based on a bad habit he is trying to change. I had a 19 year-old named Paul who came to see me because he was doing poorly in college. He had correctly assessed that he had very good academic skills, but always made excuses for himself regarding why he could not get his work done. In this case we decided his nickname would be "Mr. Excuse", and I would yell, "Mr. Excuse is in the house", every time he tried to explain his behavior away. We had a lot of fun with this, and I almost went hoarse from yelling our first 8-9 sessions. He could laugh at this and eventually he was able to "throw" this moniker off, and complete college. This was a case where giving him a negative nickname, that we agreed was fun, worked in his favor.

Lastly, if you do not believe me, try giving nicknames to adults as well. Believe me, adults love to have nicknames which describe positive things about them. Try calling your mate Sexy and see how they respond. My guess is you will be putting this book down because you will be otherwise engaged.

METAPHORS & ANALOGIES

Kids love metaphors & analogies. They are easy to understand and adolescents love to use them and create them. In addition, they provide good and memorable visual images of what you are seeking. Think about it. Is a kid more likely to remember "You did that well" or "You moved through that assignment like a bullet train through a mountain"? Of course it is more exciting if you can visualize yourself as someone who slashes through things and gets them done. This is how you want your kids to see themselves. It explains behavior, gives it a visual, and makes it far easier to remember. There are obviously countless metaphors and analogies one can use. Below are four examples from patients I have seen.

    1. Take, for example, the frequent adolescent scenario where a boy is dating one girl and is considering getting involved with his girlfriend's friend. While this is clearly morally wrong, this argument will go nowhere with adolescents. I may say to the boy "It is like we are standing on railroad tracks facing one another. There is a train coming towards you from behind, out of your sight. I can clearly see this disaster approaching and I am warning you. Unfortunately, you are looking over my shoulder and telling me the path looks completely clear. Although you see no danger, I am giving you the heads up that it is fast approaching. Your view will look totally clear right up to the point where the train runs you over (and I move off the tracks). Act now before you get crunched".

    2. Another useful one is for the adolescent who loves to have D's and F's throughout the semester only to pull them up in the end. This may work most of the time, but when it does not, it is likely to be quite costly. I tell kids, "It is as if you are walking on the edge of a cliff. It's quite exhilarating. By the way, if you are 99% successful in this endeavor - you are dead".

    3. I had a successful businessman in my office (50ish in age) who had been serially dating his whole life. He was currently concerned because he was now in the unenviable position of realizing that if he stayed on this path, he would likely grow old alone. He was dismayed that he did not see the ramifications of his lifestyle earlier. I suggested, "It was like you were dancing on a very strong wooden floor all your life. You were young, powerful and not

thinking about the future. All of a sudden it dawns on you that you may end up alone. It is as if that strong floor is deteriorating and revealing that it is actually hanging over a shark tank. The future is much scarier and riskier with this insight."

4. Many people are negative about their defenses because they are currently ruining their lives. I suggest to them that their defenses at one point were crucial to helping them get through pain and for that reason should be honored. True they are not useful now and are even destructive, but we must honor them for what they did in the past. "Your defenses are like a lifeboat which saved your life when you were drowning. Now you are on shore but insist on living in the lifeboat. This will seriously curtail your opportunities. You must now get out of the lifeboat (give up defenses that were once useful) to grow in this new place (time in your life). We can honor the lifeboat for the good it has done, but the cost of living in it now is imprisonment".

REVIEW

1. In order to be a good parent, you must have fun with your kids. Nothing is more heartwarming or bonding than enjoying each other. If I asked you to recall the best times with your parents, I am sure many of them would include fun, humor, laughter, etc. Of course, this is what brings us all together.

2. This parenting tool can be used all throughout life. I love to laugh with the people I see in therapy and I am sure it is one of the reasons they like to see me. Having fun with people allows them to loosen up, learn, and place their issues in proper perspective.

3. When you use humor and fun with your kids, it allows your kids to feel close to you and it mirrors for them the importance of enjoying life and the people you love.

4. Aside from all the 'stuff' kids have to do, it is important for parents to teach kids to learn, love and laugh. I know of no greater lesson to impart to your children than to enjoy their time while they are living on this planet.

5. One special way to increase an adolescent's self perception is to grant them a nickname. A nickname is something, which highlights an important and positive facet of who we are.

6. Nicknames should always be positive in nature (with the exception of when you have an emotionally mature adolescent who enjoys poking fun at himself, like Paul, who was discussed earlier in this chapter). They should focus on something you want to highlight or instill in an adolescent. Sometimes you will have to get creative to find something to make each adolescent unique. However it is well worth the time as kids cherish the positive nicknames they 'earn' throughout their lives.

Here are a few nicknames I have used over the years.

> NICKNAMES FOR KIDS:
> - Smarty
> - Worker Bee
> - Train
> - The Man
>
> NICKNAMES FOR ADOLESCENTS/ADULTS:
> - Warrior
> - Champion
> - Die Hard
> - Doc
> - Leader

7. Metaphors and analogies are great for adolescents. They provide a vivid picture that is easy to remember and with which they can relate. They tell an adolescent you know where he stands and you can relate. You are also telling him that there may be some serious risks he has not considered or significant positives he may glean. While an adolescent is likely to ignore straight talk regarding behavior, it is much harder to ignore a lesson wrapped in an analogy or metaphor.

CHAPTER 7

<u>FIND NICHES, BUILD NICHES, USE NICHES (IT'S ALL ABOUT NICHES)</u>

You know what really scares me during an assessment? When I ask the question "What does your child really like to do, what does he really enjoy?", and I get a blank stare. This almost always means that this adolescent has not developed any niche, any area where they feel competent, a place they feel special and alive.

This is one of the most important things with which a parent can help their child. Developing an area where a child/adolescent feels they have some competence and enjoyment is crucial to emotional health. Most children gravitate toward areas that they like. Not surprisingly, these areas are almost always ones at which they are good. However sometimes they need a little encouragement. A parent may have to try out a number of things before they hit on something their child/adolescent likes to do and at which he is good.

I believe it is a parent's responsibility to help find and nurture areas of competence – niches – that their children can enjoy as they grow through life. Take it from me, my parents put me in ice hockey at 5 and I still play 2 – 3 times per week. I loved it then, and I love it now (although my aching knees may disagree).

The rewards of this are gigantic. Not only is the child's self-esteem boosted by competence, but also these kinds of activities are usually shared with peers. From this commonality important friendships can develop. Thus, not only is your child developing a skill but his social life is expanding as well.

It is important to keep an open mind. Some adolescents may like sports, some may like artistic endeavors, some may like political involvement, etc. This is not about the parent; it is about finding a niche for your child. It never occurred to me at the time, but now I am pretty sure my mother did not want to get up at 5 AM and help tie my skates so I could play hockey. She did it because she loved me. I had a knack for it, and she wanted to be part of it. Thanks Mom.

I had a father in here many years ago that I greatly respected. He was a tremendous athlete in his day and he had a boy named Todd who he wanted to follow in his footsteps. When I met Todd, I found a nice, intelligent, but mildly depressed 13 year-old. Upon assessment it became clear that Todd did not value athletics, was poor at them, and had just jumped to a developmental milestone where he could correctly assess that he was not a good athlete. To compound matters, his father was still very good at all sports and was often approached by people who commented on his skill level.

Todd's father was very direct and noted how he enjoyed being a good athlete. His two themes were that it brought him a lot of happiness and it brought him most of his lifelong friends. He wanted his son to experience both of these joys.

The father was also quite sharp. He could see that his son did not have his abilities, or even the ability to compete with his own age group.

What he did next really earned my respect. Without his son saying anything, he went out and bought him a violin (a hobby he knew his son loved). He wanted to give his child a different venue to reach the same goals. Five years later that child became the lead chair in one of the best music groups in the State. His demeanor was noticeably positive as he correctly assessed he was quite a good violinist. Not surprisingly he developed many good friends who were involved in music as well. This father gave his son the opportunity to shine; he was not stuck on the source of that opportunity.

BUILDING ON A NICHE

Let's look at an example of what I mean. A father (Max) was estranged from his 14 year-old son (Sam) and came to my office for help. He was divorced and only saw his son a few times every few weeks. He was very concerned that his ex-wife was alienating his son from him. Upon assessment I could see this was far from the case. In fact, Sam wanted to have a relationship with his dad and his ex-wife was supporting it (in part because she wanted some free time for herself as well). So what was the problem?

Dad was the problem. He was a car enthusiast. He loved all cars and loved what they did. His passion had actually contributed to his divorce because of the amount of time and money he spent on this hobby. Sam was not so much into cars. He loved baseball and was quite a player. Dad thought baseball was boring and wanted to 'train' his son to love cars.

So every other weekend Sam would go to his dad's house where his dad would have planned an event revolving around cars, e.g., car shows, car expos, etc. The dad's natural inclination was noble, he wanted to share his passion with his son. However, Sam was giving his dad a road map to his heart and it was not through pit row – it was through baseball. Most kids will tell you how to get to them. They are not good at playing it coy. It is a parent's job to listen and respond. Sam was saying 'here is the map' and Dad was saying 'I do not care what the map says, I know the way'. Ouch!

If Dad wanted a relationship with his son he should start bringing him to baseball games and attending his son's games. Is this fair? Who cares? It works. Inevitably if Dad bends first, eventually, Sam will end up at a car show with his dad and their relationship will improve dramatically.

During a session, after Dad had learned to read the road map, I asked what they had done one weekend. Dad said they had gone to a car show. I glanced at Dad thinking he had taken a step back. Sam jumped in and told me that he had asked to go and he really enjoyed it. The point is that when Sam was not forced to go every weekend to car shows, and Dad showed real interest in Sam's sport, Sam became much more open to Dad's hobby.

So Dad's idea about alienation was changed to realizing that his son was not a car enthusiast (a tough pill to swallow). However, the responsibility for having a relationship rested in Dad's lap and he picked it up.

You were a kid once and you had the option to choose what you were going to like and do. It is the same with your child. They get to choose, and you as a parent, get to follow (if you want a good relationship with your children).

Sacrifice is an important part of parenting, as is supporting. Get used to it and do not let your selfish or even misguided noble desires steer you wide of a relationship with your child.

REVIEW

1. There are few things more important in life than developing a niche. This is an area of competence which brings you pleasure and in which you are skilled.

2. It is sometimes difficult for parents to understand that their child/adolescent is not a mini replica of themselves. What was your niche may very well not be your adolescent's niche.

3. Most parents (by the time they become parents) have had successes in various areas. They usually want to pass these down to their offspring. This is great. However, sometimes children/adolescents will develop skill sets in areas far removed from their parents' skills (as in the chapter example of an adolescent loving music while his father was an athlete).

4. It is important that parents watch their children to see where their natural inclinations take them. Adolescents will be good at those activities they like. And those activities they like are usually the ones at which they are proficient.

5. If you want to build a good relationship with your adolescent, join them in the things they are good at rather than insisting they become good at the things you may like.

CHAPTER 8

<u>RISK TAKING CAN BE GOOD</u>

Far too many parents try to protect their kids from every little hurt. Support your kid taking risks – even if they are in over their heads. Winning, losing, and learning are by-products of taking chances (again, not insane chances). Understand that the kids who take chances are the ones who will do more with their lives.

I have seen thousands of adolescents in my career. It is not the hell-raiser who concerns me, but the adolescent who sits stoically in my office almost too afraid to breathe. The hell-raiser will get into plenty of trouble, but most of the time will not only figure it out, but will thrive. The fearful one, where does he go to learn? Unfortunately, he goes nowhere and does not learn. Instead, he walls himself off from everything and is never able to get out of his own shell.

I laugh with parents when they tell me they are confused about how this 'little bundle of joy' they picked up at the hospital became this gnarly 16 year-old who is getting into all sorts of trouble. My belief is that if hospitals really wanted to be proactive, they would place a tag on the toe of these little 'bundles of joy' that says something like 'your cute little baby will change in approximately 12 years at which time he/she will evolve into an alien who is likely to go toilet papering, pool hopping, and be brought home by the police at least once – Enjoy'.

Believe it or not, this is not all bad news. You want your child to push the envelope once in awhile. Shedler & Block (1990) ran a longitudinal study looking at how people turned out in their 30's and compared it to their level of drug usage in high school. They broke the high schoolers into three groups: never tried, experimenters, and frequent users. What they found was that in their thirties one of the groups was doing very poorly. They were experiencing interpersonal alienation, poor impulse control, and various other signs of emotional distress. Can you guess which group that was? It was the frequent users who never really became better adjusted.

However, they also found another group, which was not doing so well. This group was characterized by anxiety, being emotionally restricted and showing poor social skills. This was the never tried group. That's right; never trying drugs was a predictor for poor adjustment later in this study. The last group, the experimenters who gave up drug usage, were the most well adjusted.

This research does not mean you should rush out and tell your adolescents to experiment with drugs. Drug usage is NOT good. But it does highlight that being afraid to take any risks in life is likely a marker for poor adjustment. The adolescents who tried drugs and then decided it was not for them did the best. Again, they were willing to take a risk, but not get too involved when they saw the consequences. These people were the ones who continued to take risks and were able to differentiate which ones were worthwhile and which ones were not.

I don't tell this to adolescents because I know what I will hear, but parents should understand the ramifications of this. The study is far less about smoking marijuana and far more about taking some risks in life. This is why when parents are very upset about their child trying marijuana; I try to ease their minds a bit by letting them know that their adolescent may be well adjusted and just experimenting. Look at the depth of problems their usage brings to their lives, not just the action itself.

Risk taking is the springboard into life. It is easy to stay safe. I play hockey and intermittently I will get injured (as I am writing this book I am recovering from knee surgery). People will ask why I don't just stop playing. I tell them I love it too much to ever stop playing. I consider the injuries the price I pay to continue to play.

They are not APART FROM the game but A PART OF the game and if you do not want to pay that price, you should not play.

I could play and assure myself I will never be injured. All I have to do is wear so many pads that it would be impossible to hurt me. I mean I could get covered head to toe and be entirely in my own protective bubble. However, if I choose this route, I am unlikely to ever touch the puck again, receive a pass or score a goal. In essence, keeping myself safe from injury would also keep me from enjoying the game. Risk and injury are part of the game as they are part of life.

Risk taking is an essential feature of life. When my kids fall playing (ages 5 & 7) I hug them and tell them I will help them, but I also tell them that falling is part of playing. You will stumble sometimes, and I don't want that to be the focus of your play. I want them to enjoy themselves but also understand that there will be a price to pay every once in a while and I expect them to understand that or to stop playing (impossible for my kids).

One of the examples of learning from error is looking at a tennis player like Roger Federer. He is arguably the greatest tennis player to ever play the game. Now guess who has hit more balls out of the court – him or me. He has, of course. Each error he has made on the court has made him a better player. He became better and better at hitting just inside the lines by learning from his near misses. Those players who were afraid to go for the lines never learned to hit just inside them. They played it safe and are high probability players who always keep the ball in court. Unfortunately, they will never reach the highest levels of the game where hitting very near the line differentiates the good from the great. Because Roger allowed himself to take more risks and make more mistakes, he became one of the greatest athletes of our generation. Remember, taking risks can be the best teacher of all.

Lastly, I have taught many kids to skate. One of the things that parents always question me about is that during the first practice I do a drill where every time I blow the whistle I want the kids to fall to the ice and get up. "Why are you teaching them to fall, I brought them here to learn to skate" I will hear. The answer is obvious. I do not want the kids to fear falling and once they have mastered falling and getting up they will not fear it. I do this so they will skate harder and take more risks. Yes, that will lead to more falling but it will also lead them to fine tune their skating, turning, and reduce injuries to the point where they can fly on the ice. Those kids, who fear falling, and never want to fall, will never really extend themselves to become good skaters or players.

This lesson can be seen in almost every endeavor in life. If you are willing to push the limits and take some risks you will probably be quite good at what you are trying.

REVIEW

1. Risk taking is a necessary part of any successful life. The trick is understanding which risks are worth taking and which involve too great a cost.

2. For those who fear risk, or worse yet, never want to experience failure, life will be a long road of getting what others give to you rather than creating your own future.

3. The adolescents who scare me most are the ones who sit passively and let life run them over. They say little, do little, and are too afraid to take any chances in the real world. The hell-raisers are more likely to come to the attention of the authorities, but they are also more likely to take the kind of risks that move people forward.

CHAPTER 9

ALL ROADS START WITH THE GOOD

BUILD ON THE GOOD

Go to my website (www.drdugganandassociates.com) and read about our practice. It is about positives, strengths and how we need to tune into them and nurture them with our kids. "But I thought psychologists worked on problems". No, I do not. I work with kids on their issues and I am betting that 80% – 90% of who your child is, is not a problem. I support these strengths and I let each child know that they are much bigger than their 'problem'. The problem itself is usually just one small facet of who they are.

Another thing which is important for people to realize is that in therapy, as in life, I want to work with the person most capable of making the most change and affecting the most change. "But I thought you worked with problem people". No, I work with solution people.

Sometimes that will be the child, sometimes a parent, sometimes another relative. The only cases that I see as truly challenging are when I interview a family and see no area of health, no person who can affect positive change. When this occurs, I have no one to bring into therapy and build upon so I have to roll up my sleeves and find slivers of good elsewhere.

Parents always give me a quizzical look when I tell them the first session I want their adolescent to bring in something positive, something they are proud of, something they can share and brag about. It is by tuning into what they do well that they will find the tools to change their troubling behavior. If an adolescent can acknowledge and learn about their own strengths, they can bring these to bear on their current circumstances. We all improve by using our strengths to overcome our weaknesses.

I like all my patients, especially the children, to get to know what they do well. Parents need to spend time each day helping kids to learn what they do well. It is these skills that will get them out of a jam and lead them to new heights. Understanding their strengths, and enlarging them, is what leads people to be successful. Certainly we do not want kids to spend all their time worried about their weaknesses or their weaknesses will become them.

People become what they spend their time on. If your child spends his time creating and appreciating his skills, he will use them throughout his life. We all know someone who rattles on and on about the same problem year after year. He has become that problem. When you think of that person you think of the problem. I heard a wise priest once say succinctly, "What you cannot forgive, and therefore dwell upon, becomes a part of you". I am also sure you know someone who spends most of their time focused on the good things in their lives (this is a trait my mother has). You probably enjoy interacting with this person. You can be that person.

Families who support each other's strengths tend to be healthier and more firmly grounded. One clear example of this comes from when you assess children of divorce. Despite all the hype, which suggests that divorce hurts children, this is not substantiated by research. Rather, what injures children most is not the divorce, but the acrimony between parents. Children who are brought up by divorced parents who get along, are far better off psychologically than those who develop in an intact family where the parents are unkind and cruel toward each other. It is the attitude that children live with which provides their foundation – not who is in the house.

If you want a concrete example of what to do, remember to point out one or two positives about your kids each day to them. It is not one or two drops of rain which make a person wet, it is the steady stream of rain which douses us. Do this with your children and they will learn to love their strengths.

In most of my patient's homes, I suggest putting up a large white board. On the board will be various things like chores, things to do this week, etc. I also suggest that part of the board have your children's names listed, and below the names, list some qualities you admire about them such as kind, honest, giving, good listener, nice to sibling, etc. There are endless attributes you can place here. If you change them every once in a while, your children will look forward to reading what you write. In addition, you can ask your children what qualities they admire and those can be part of it too.

CATCH THEM BEING GOOD

Another skill, which is awfully fun to do, is catch your child/adolescent being good. We all know how to catch kids misbehaving. In fact, as parents we often spend a lot more time in this endeavor than in catching them being good. When your child/adolescent does something you think is good, stop and comment on it. Comments like "Hey that was really nice of you to help your sister" mean a lot to kids. Sometimes you might even want to reward them for it. Things like "Hey, I noticed you helped your Mom without being asked. That is great. Would you like to go out and get a dessert?" This kind of thing gets kids to notice what they are doing. It also lets them know you are noticing. Adults love this too. Don't you like it when people notice the good things you do? Well so does your adolescent.

I will end this chapter with an exception to this rule. If your child suffers from a severe psychopathology, then just building on their strengths will not be enough. It will certainly be part of the puzzle, but medications and a structured environment may also be necessary to achieve positive change. In the Chapter 'Severe Psychiatric Issues', I cover this topic in greater depth. However, even with a child who may have a deeper pathology, it is important to stress his good qualities, as these will be the skills he uses to further himself throughout life.

REVIEW

1. The question is 'How do adolescents get better and learn'? The answer is they focus on what they do well and do more of it.

2. If you focus on your adolescent's strengths you will probably get more of that behavior. Conversely, if you focus on the negative get ready for more of that behavior.

3. We all become what we spend our time on.

4. Let your adolescent know what you see as their assets and strengths and listen to them as they tell you what they believe they can do well.

5. Catch your adolescent being good and let them know you see and value what they do.

6. You do not move forward in life by squashing parts of your personality that you do not like. You move forward by concentrating on the areas of your life where you excel and using these skills to work on the areas where you have greater difficulties.

7. It is important for parents to help their adolescent find and nurture their strengths. When an adolescent feels good about areas of his life he is likely to spend more times in these areas. As a parent, support your adolescent's skills (even if they are not what you would have chosen) and let him know you see his strengths.

8. It is our strengths that help us achieve in life, not our weaknesses.

CHAPTER 10

BE A LEADER

This is hard for a lot of parents and I understand why. It is tough to be a leader when the troops want to rebel. Double the difficulty when you really want the troops to love you. Is that an excuse to not lead? No. It is just an understanding.

Can you tolerate adolescent anger and conflict? Is it worth it to be respected and have your adolescent understand who runs the show? This is for you to decide. I will say I have NEVER seen a house run well where an adolescent is in charge.

What most parents want here is for adolescents to understand and go along (I do). However, a river flows in one direction because the banks hold firm and move the water that way. You are the banks of your family and no matter what the unruly water does, you must stay strong.

The foundations you lay as parents develop family strength. It does not have to be intrusive but it must be strong when it needs to be.

Here are some arrows your adolescent will fling your way (along with a rating of their effectiveness from 1 – 10).

1. Your adolescent 'hates' you today (7). It would garner a higher score except that it happens so often. Adolescents are very emotional and do not like 'no' so they do a lot of brooding. The angst of that brooding is usually you, so get used to it. This too shall pass, and allowing it to affect you only strengthens it.

2. Your adolescent insists you don't understand when you just don't agree (4). The reason this is so low is that this is usually a power play by your adolescent. They almost always know why you do not agree, but they are just attempting to get you into a discussion where they can use other methods to get their ways. It is

OK to let them know you have differing opinions. That is not the end of the world.

3. Your adolescent wishes he had his friend's parents - they are sooooo cool (1). This is usually good for a laugh and a suggestion that he interviews those parents and see what they are willing to offer to someone who is 15, in school, rarely cleans up after himself, uses a lot of money...and I almost forgot – does not have a job.

The point here is that you do not have to respond. I am constantly amazed by the number of times parents tell me their kids are argumentative. What this usually means is the parent wants the adolescent to agree with something and the adolescent wants to argue. You do not need agreement. You need compliance – that is all. If you stop talking there will be no argument.

It is hard to disappoint your child, but it is part of parenting. This is a place where having a supportive spouse pays off. I had a parent ask me recently if she should let her 16 year-old, who is battling a major drug problem, go to an all night concert in another city. Is that question for real? The parent knows the answer; she just wants me to be the bad guy instead of her. Parents are the pilots of their family. When you hit turbulence, do you want the cockpit door to open and have the pilot take a survey of what to do – or do you want them to just take charge and land the plane?

It is crucial that parents not fear being the 'bad guy'. Sometimes it is necessary. I remember when I was in my training. I saw a patient and had to make a difficult decision with which the mom disagreed. The cost of not doing it would have left the child extremely vulnerable and in danger. The mom was angry with me and I felt horrible since I liked both her and her child. I remember my supervisor saying "You won't always feel good after making the right decision, but you have to know it is in the best interest of the person under your care". In the case of adolescents it is important to remember that although they may disagree, they will conform about 90% of the time if the leader is strong, benevolent, does listen, is respectful, and does not ask to be agreed with all the time.

On the adolescent drug unit, I remember that the adolescents wanted to go out to a head shop (place where drug paraphernalia is sold) on New Year's Eve. They insisted they would stay sober but they did not want to be cooped up on New Year's Eve. I said no. When they began to discuss it with me, I had them acknowledge that I was open and truthful with them, had allowed them many privileges, was always honest with them, and listened to them. They agreed and then I told them I was pulling rank here and making a decision I knew would be unpopular, but I was asking them to go with it considering all the other things we had been through. This worked here and the issue was solved (by the way if they had disagreed the decision would have been the same, but they would have had a harder time with it).

There is also a very important upside to being a leader in your family. There will be times when you can be a teacher that your adolescent never forgets. A poignant example happened for me at 14 when my father took me to the racetrack. I loved to go to the horse races and we had some wonderful times betting our two dollars on the ponies. The thirty minutes between races allowed plenty of time to talk about anything or everything. On this particular day, we were on the bottom floor. This floor has approximately twenty doors placed together which lead to the rail of the track. While we were there, it started to rain. My father promptly got up, closed the middle 18 doors leaving two doors, one at each end, open. He then asked me to get on the escalator, which we took to the third floor. As we were going up he told me he never wanted me to follow the crowd for the sake of following the crowd. I thought that was a strange to say right then. However, when we got to the top level, he asked me to look over the railing at the track below. I could not believe it, there were about 300 people WAITING IN LINE to get into one of the open doors. My dad told me all the doors were open but that no one dared to step out of line to challenge the shut doors. No one had to get wet if they just left the line and attempted to walk through the shut doors. No one did – it was an unbelievable visual, which is etched in my mind. My father turned to me and said, "Never be afraid to reach out, or jump out of line. Be who you are and feel free to challenge when you think it can be of benefit". I have never forgotten the lesson or the visual. That is leadership. That is teaching.

This is also one of those skills which works better in adolescence if you have built your credibility in prior years. I remember being out with a friend of mine who had a very cute, and precocious, 8 year-old, named Zach. Zach's dad was very straight-forward and had no problem following through on his word. Zach loved to challenge his Dad. One day, when we were eating, Zach pulled a golf ball out of his pocket. His dad said, "Do not put that ball in your mouth. If it touches your lips we will get up and go home and you will not be going outside today". Zach then took the ball, put it at arm's length and slowly moved it toward his mouth at a very slow pace. His dad did not flinch and actually hardly seemed to notice. As Zach approached his mouth, I thought there was going to be trouble. When he was microscopically away from his lips he stopped. His dad said "You can keep the ball right there or eat your food. It's up to you". Zach put the ball down and that was that. The dad knew Zach liked to challenge the rules (just like a lot of 8 year olds). Likewise, Zach knew Dad's word was law and would be followed. He was clearly a leader in the family. No fighting, just fact. Well done Dad.

REVIEW

1. Being a leader in your family is often difficult, but always rewarding. Remember the raging river wants to run wild (this is your adolescent). It is the strong banks of the river, which channel it in one direction (Guess who this is?).

2. Adolescents are not at a point in their lives where they can always make competent, proactive decisions. They tend to make decisions based on short-term thinking and emotion as well as limited knowledge.

3. Allowing your adolescent to make decisions in situations of limited consequence is good training. However, it is important that parents watch the bigger decisions and intercede when necessary.

4. Many times adolescents believe they are on equal ground with their parents. This is a dangerous idea to cultivate. Parents are the leaders in the family and should accept this mantle and live it.

5. It is OK if an adolescent is rebellious and objects to authority. It is the parent's responsibility to not give in to this kind of manipulation.

6. Understand that sometimes your feelings will be hurt as your child attempts to get their way. That hurt should be a reminder to you of the depth of love for your child AND that you are doing the right thing.

10 TRAPS PARENTS SHOULD AVOID

CHAPTER 1

HOW TO RAISE A TEENZILLA

I know, I know. I have been writing about how important it is to lead with positives and now I am writing a chapter primarily focused on what not to do. However, it is just too easy and fun to write this chapter so I am breaking the rules and going with it anyway. I am not going to go into great detail on each behavior. I think you will see how each of these behaviors (and there are many more) could lead your child from cute youngster to Teenzilla. If you see yourself in any of these, put the book down, slowly move away from the couch, and change this instant.

1. *Don't Ever Listen to your Adolescent* - He is just a kid and what could he know anyway. This goes along with such behaviors as constantly interrupting your adolescent when he wants to say something, belittling his ideas, and ignoring his ideas. When you do not listen to your adolescent, you tell him he is unimportant and unintelligent. This type of behavior leads to an adolescent who will not talk to you and will harbor negative feelings about you. But don't worry; you'll never know this because you will be doing all the talking and none of the listening.

2. *Never Engage your Adolescent in a Discussion about Anything Meaningful.* This way your adolescent will learn you do not like to talk about these subjects and he will get all his ideas from the television or the Internet or his same aged friends. We all know how helpful advice from those three sources can be.

3. *When your Adolescent has an Excuse For Their irresponsible Behavior – Buy It Hook, Line and Sinker*. This goes perfectly with allowing your adolescent to make the same error time and time again without there being any serious consequences for them. If there is ever a way to undermine personal responsibility, this is it. Whether you are too lazy to parent or just do not want to take the heat, allow your adolescent to BS you with some excuse and then

consider the case closed. If you do this enough your adolescent will learn this is very effective. Hopefully, he will try it out in the real world where he will be stunned by the consequences he will endure.

4. *Give, Give, Give, Give, Give…….and then Give Some More.* Whatever your precious wants or needs, please give it to him immediately. Having to work for rewards is just too much of a hassle. Earning rewards is overrated. Your job is to provide for their every possible need. Apologize when you are unable to meet all of his needs. Hopefully, he will forgive you for this oversight. He will enter the real world with the idea that everyone should take care of him. And I think we all know how that will play out.

5. *Tell Your Adolescent What He Wants To Hear Instead Of What He Needs To Hear.* This will significantly reduce your need to spend any energy parenting. Whatever your kid wants to do is fine and tell them so. Big deal if he breaks curfew. So what if he blows dope in your basement. He'll grow out of it and if he doesn't? Well he can sack out in the basement until he is 40.

6. *Be Grumpy and Depressed Most Of The Time.* I know you probably love to be around depressed and grumpy people – who doesn't? And you probably have some good reason that you tell yourself like 'I work hard so I have a right to spew my negativity all around'. This will be quite attractive to your adolescent. Don't worry about having to clean your home for visitors, your adolescent's friends will never come over and eventually neither will your adolescent.

7. *Please Do Not Allow Your Adolescent To Take Any Risks.* He may get hurt you know. Hopefully you can coddle and cradle him until he is 18 and then let him out into the real world. Be sure to always run interference for him with his teachers. Heck, why stop there? If a professor gives your precious a poor grade, call the university. If your darling's boss is being unfair, go down to that office. Just whatever you do, make sure he is 100% coddled and his life is risk-free.

8. *When Parenting Spend Most Of Your Time Pointing Out Errors*. Any time not spent on this should be focused on looking for more negatives for when you see your adolescent again………which will be in about two years. Get a big sign that says 'Punish Hard, Praise Never'.

9. *Don't Help Your Child Discover Those Things They Do Well.* Helping kids to discover what they do well will only lead to your adolescent being involved in activities, which are positive and brings them friends. It will come with the added down side of more work for you. Avoid at all costs.

10. *Lecture, Lecture, Lecture…But Never Act.* What really helps kids is to hear the same talk over and over. That glazed, far off look you see in your adolescent's eyes signals rapt attention to whatever you are preaching. That yawning says you are getting through. Kids love it when parents talk because that usually means nothing of real consequence is going to happen.

11. *Respect Your Child's Privacy Above All Other Things*. To be successful here one must avoid all common sense. Never look into what he is doing. If he is on the Internet, that is his time. If he is in his room with a member of the opposite sex and the door is closed, that's their business. That way if he is talking to someone who is a bad influence, or is engaged in dangerous or destructive behaviors, you will not have to know about it. What a relief.

12. *Become Totally Enmeshed With Your Adolescent*. Remember how tough it was for you to negotiate the waters of adolescence; the constant ups and downs, the crises, the learning about relationships – good and bad. How about the hormonal and physical changes? Good times. Well, heck, let's take that ride again, this time in the shoes of your adolescent. Whenever he goes through something, you should jump in emotionally and go through it as well. When his boat is rocked, do not stand strong on the shore showing him the way, get right into the boat and let it rock your

world too. Spend as much time worrying as any other teenager. Who needs to parent when you can be an adolescent again.

13. *More Of The Same* – When, as a parent, things are not working, do not consider changing tactics or re-evaluating what you are doing. Instead, tell yourself that whether your actions are working or not, you are going to stubbornly do the same thing. In fact you are not going to just do the same thing, you are going to do it more. This usually leads to getting more of the same result….which is not working. Don't get creative or decide to change the way you are acting – just do more of the same. Nice job 'Oh Stubborn One'.

REVIEW

1. While there are many more, these are the top dozen (plus one) ways to screw up your adolescent.

2. All of us (parents) fall into these traps. It is the parents who live this way that ultimately warp their adolescent. If you are doing any of these, stop right now.

3. Although I have written this chapter in a humorous, tongue-in-cheek manner, it is not funny to see an adolescent who has grown up under some of these principles. These adolescents are usually on the way to becoming handicapped, dysfunctional adults who are out of sync with how the world works. As a parent you have the power to change today – DO IT!

CHAPTER 2

ADOLESCENT SEE – ADOLESCENT DO

WHAT YOU DO IS WORTH SO MUCH MORE THAN WHAT YOU SAY

It doesn't take a genius to know this is true. Let's just look at one behavior, smoking. Did you know that if you smoke there is a significantly higher chance that your child will smoke? This seems like a no brainer, but I am shocked at the number of parents who seem surprised by it. Each and every year I will get the following story from a kid:

Dr. Matt: Why are you smoking pot?

Adolescent: Cause I like to.

Dr. Matt: Your parents are sending you here to help you stop.

Adolescent: Yeah, right. My mom has it stashed in her dresser – I steal it from there all the time...

There is little that can be done in this case. You can rationalize, moralize, demonize, tell the kids you are the parent, etc., but if you are engaging in the same behavior you want your kid to stop, there is going to be trouble.

Parents fool themselves by telling themselves stories to make themselves feel good. I had a patient who complained about her daughter's promiscuity. The girl, Angie, was 16 and 'involved' with just about every boy in school.

When I met Angie, she was cute and open and said she thought her behavior was fine until she found out how many people were making fun of her, and that her reputation was that of a 'slut'. She seemed genuinely surprised by this because she was outgoing, a good student and viewed herself as a nice kid.

When we discussed her behavior, she could see what she was doing and began to consider it a problem. When I asked how she became so involved with boys, she let me know she had not even kissed a boy before freshman year. However, she said she did not see the difference between what her mom was doing and what she was doing.

Her mother was an attractive, divorced mother of 4 who had been 'dating' the last 6 years or so. Her dating life consisted of finding older, well-to-do gentlemen who knew how to pay for vacations, cars, dinners, events, etc. Her daughter could see that these men were 'pleased' by Mom. While engaging in this kind of behavior she would make sure to tell her daughter that these 'boyfriends' were not to be respected or considered a potential partner. You can see what happened. The daughter was trading favors with boys as she had learned from watching her mom.

What was worse was that when I discussed this with the mom, she had convinced herself that what she was doing was fine. She had created a life 'story' to shield her from taking responsibility for her life. She was not a prostitute – she was simply accepting the kind things that men would do for her. When the cash was cut off by one, well she was not prostituting herself; she was just getting together with another 'new friend' who happened to be wealthy and would give her gifts, money, etc. Basically, she was acting like a prostitute regardless of what she told herself or her daughter. Not surprisingly, her daughter was acting the same way.

Remember, your adolescent is not listening to the fable you are telling yourself, what they are watching is your behavior.

Similarly, I had a father who came to me because his 17 year-old son was in a one year old relationship with his first serious girlfriend. He noted that his son, Mark, was treating this girl very poorly. He often called her names, had asked her friend out while they were dating, and made fun of her when she was not around. Surprisingly, he told his dad he 'loved' her and did not want the relationship to end. The dad asked if I could help. Realizing that most adolescents learn how to treat the opposite gender by how their parents treat each other I asked about how he and his wife got along. I was told in no uncertain terms that Marks' mom was his EX-WIFE. I then got an earful regarding what a B---- his ex-wife is. He used the most degrading and base language I have ever heard by a patient to describe his ex-wife. When I asked if his kids had heard him speak like this, he said "Of course, I am a good father and I am always honest with my kids". As I worked with Mark I soon realized he was parroting his father's actions. Although his father stated he wanted Mark to be good to his girlfriend, Mark's father was as verbally degrading to his ex-wife as anyone I have ever encountered. Not surprisingly, Mark followed his dad's behavior, not his advice.

Lastly, let me tell you about an example in my own life regarding my father. My family is generally very expressive. However, my dad is quite 'old school' and so saying things like "I love you" did not come easily to him. Fortunately for him, he married my mom who is extremely open and expressive and so there were a lot of "I Love You's" in our home. So you might say to yourself 'Poor Dr. Matt, his father did not tell him he loved him a lot'. If you think this, you are in error. That's because my father did not have to say it – he showed it all the time. When there was an important game I was playing in, I could count on looking down to the end of the rink and seeing a silver haired man in a large coat watching intensely. If I needed something for school or sports, I knew I had to ask only once and there it would be. After my dad came home from a long day at work, if I wanted friends to come over, I barely ever heard 'no'. I remember in my early twenties when my sight suddenly began to deteriorate, I went to the doctor to have it tested. It was scary for me and for the rest of my family. When I emerged from the doctor's office, I looked up to see that silver haired fellow sitting in his car in the parking lot. I asked what he was doing and he said, "Oh, is this where your doctor works? I was just driving around and decided to take a rest". We had a good laugh and he asked what the doctor had said. I was (and still am) my dad's kid and he was worried and wanted to be there for me. Now I could tell you similar stories regarding my mom, but this chapter is about doing rather than saying and she was great at both.

So let me ask you, would you rather have someone who says they love you or someone who shows you they love you? Saying is nice; doing is what imprints on people. So my advice is shut up and put up – that makes all the difference in the world.

REVIEW

1. Your adolescent is a full time learning machine. He or she is taking in everything you say and do and trying to understand it.

2. Adolescents often mimic the behaviors they see from their parents.

3. It does not matter much what you say to your adolescent, the sound of your actions will always trump your words.

4. If you are doing something you do not want your adolescent to do; why you are doing it is insignificant (this is the story you are telling yourself to justify your actions). You can bank on your adolescent following your behavior not your words.

5. If you want your child/adolescent to live a certain way, make sure you are living that way.

CHAPTER 3

YOUR ADOLESCENT HAS ENOUGH FRIENDS - BE A PARENT

Many parents become frustrated because kids and adolescents just do not want to follow the rules. They complain, barter, and negotiate, etc. to get around rules that seem obvious to their parents. What the parents are not appreciating is that the job of a kid is to push on the rules to see which really apply and which are just a smokescreen. It is the parent's response, which tells the adolescent how important the rules are and if the parent should be heeded.

Let's look at an example from my case files:

Dr. Matt: Mr. Marx, I wanted to call and discuss your son Jake's (age 17) progress in therapy.

Mr. Marx: Great, thank you.

Dr. Matt: I really enjoy Jake as a kid. I mean he's 17, a good kid, not real serious about school, but overall a pretty kind-hearted young man. However, he says he does not want to stop smoking pot and he seems very cavalier when I tell him that you are invested in his stopping.

Mr. Marx: Hmmm.

Dr. Matt: I think either we should have a family meeting where we let him know, in no uncertain terms, what is going to happen to him if he keeps smoking, or I think you may be wasting your money sending him to see me. He likes me I know, but he seems unconcerned about the consequences I am going to suggest we follow.

Mr. Marx: Thank you for your honesty Dr. Matt, but I don't think this is all your fault.

Dr. Matt: What do you mean? You are sending him to me and we are not getting the results we agreed upon. I think maybe a change in direction is warranted.

Mr. Marx: Well, before we do that I have a little confession to make. He is a great kid and I do want him to stop smoking pot. However, we both love to play basketball so whenever we go out to play (which is about once or twice a month) we smoke out afterwards and talk about the game.

Dr. Matt: SILEEEEEEEEEEEEEENCE. UH-HUH. So you are sending him to me to help him stop smoking dope, but you are smoking with him once or twice a month? I can see why he may not be stopping and he is not afraid of you punishing him. You realize that, whether he likes me or not, I am just his therapist – you are his PARENT and no one is more important than you.

Great kid and a dad who really wants to be 'cool', but the problem is obvious. Of course therapy is going to be ineffective when a father is smoking pot with his son, while telling his son he should not do it. In fact, the entire smoking issue is a symbol of how the father treats his son. The dad wants desperately to be hanging out and having fun with his 'friend' so he is willing to suspend all his rules, especially those that make him look 'uncool', in order to garner favor with his son. What he does not realize is that this one incident then allows his son to discount all the advice his dad has given him. Is it any wonder that he was completely non-phased by my assertion that his dad was going to punish him for his behavior? Yeah right! He knew far better than I did, he just did not want to narc on his dad.

The ending to this particular story was entirely foreseeable and quite sad. Jake, who had many gifts, drifted into heavier drug usage. He failed to graduate from high school after he was found with pot on him at school and expelled. Even after that he continued to smoke pot and eventually his father sent him out of state to a residential setting in order to help him simply graduate from high school – a feat well within his abilities. The last I heard he was working on a farm in the Midwest........still smoking pot.

When parents give up their roles as parents, they are really cutting their kids adrift. Kids need firm direction especially when they are dealing in the world of adolescent decision-making. When a parent abdicates this role, it is like putting a sailboat in the water and taking off the rudder (and maybe throwing in a tornado as well). Who knows where the boat is going to end up?

Another consequence of a parent violating his own rules is that it causes the adolescent to lose respect for the parent. You may think you are being 'cool', but the fact is that adolescents know when you are this needy and use it to validate their own misbehaviors. And if you think you can step out of this role and enforce some discipline in some areas, you are in for a rude awakening. This kind of deviation from the norm will result in your child ignoring pretty much anything you have to say. Why shouldn't they just do whatever they want? Why should they listen to you – you're just a big kid.

Lastly, as was seen here, when the most powerful figures of your life are so easily corrupted, you tend to think all institutional rules are malleable. Hence you begin to make mistakes in other arenas where the rules do not change. In this case Jake began to bring drugs to school. When he was caught the principal did not consider smoking with him. Rather, he expelled Jake. This must have come as quite a shock to Jake because the principal actually liked him. I let him know it is not the liking that keeps you in school; you also have to be accountable. His Parent/friend neglected to teach him this.

I see this at all different levels of parenting but I do not think it is ever more destructive than in adolescence.

Let's look at another example from the files of Dr. Matt. While I was the Director of Services at a large Adolescent Chemical Dependency Unit (unit for adolescents dealing with drug problems), we had a 16 year-old female on the unit. As is sometimes the case with 16 year-old females, she had physically matured very early and appeared more like 24. She was extremely well developed and attractive, and was well aware of it. In fact, one of the reasons she had a drug problem is that older men would fall over themselves giving this girl free drugs in the belief that it would lead to an adventurous evening with her.

Therapy was going well with her, as she was quite open as to how she had been using her sexuality to support her habit. A problem we encountered occurred when we took the adolescents to a morning meeting. At this meeting there were adults as well. Almost every day we would have to fend off an attempt or two to get to know her by someone in their 20's or 30's.

In family therapy, we worked with her single mother on setting better limits for her daughter, especially as it came to her sexuality. Helping this 16 year-old be 16 and act 16 would go a long way in helping her back into a mainstream peer group and onto a more productive life. After all, there would be plenty of time for her to be 24 when she was 24.

As luck would have it she celebrated her 17th birthday on our unit. We were going to have a small party for her and asked her mother to come. Her mother did and she brought a gift. The mother entered her daughter's room and about 15 minutes later the girl jumped out of her room wearing the skimpiest mini skirt I have ever seen with her makeup all done, exclaiming "Look what my mom gave me, wait till those boys on the adult unit see me now". Behind her stood a beaming mother saying, "I knew she really wanted it, so I got it for her"!!!

I pulled the mother aside to express my disappointment that she was again pushing her daughter toward a lifestyle she was too emotionally immature to handle. To my amazement the mother said, "Oh, I think you are right, but she would have been mad if I didn't get her something like this, and I hate it when she is mad at me".

We told mom to take the mini-mini-mini-skirt home (all two inches of it). Therapy went well while she was on our unit and we eventually discharged Lynn. Lynn did not stay in touch with the unit, and I fear the night she got out her "friend" (Mom) bought her some very sexy outfits and took her out on the town.

While these two examples are stark and easy to see, it is important for every parent to remember that they are their child's guide in life. It is far more important that a parent says what has to be said than what their adolescent wants to hear. It is hard to say no and know your child is angry. But when you lay down at night, it is far better to believe your child is angry with you than it is to think that you might be supporting, and even encouraging, him down a path of disappointment and pain.

I have saved the best story for last, and it is one I still have trouble wrapping my head around. Again, when I was Director of Services of the Chemical Dependency Unit, we often had very challenging adolescents on our unit. I had a tremendous therapeutic team and we prided ourselves on being able to reach most, if not all, of the kids sent to us. There was one young man named Steve who was especially manipulative. Now do not get me wrong, it is often good to be able to manipulate your world. However, Steve had really worked this to perfection. He had convinced his father that he should have a large allowance, be able to stay out as long as he wanted, and as long as he did not get arrested, be able to use narcotics. When I questioned the father on this arrangement, he spoke a lot about his own guilt having divorced Steve's mom and causing Steve 'to grow up with no mother figure in his life'. Dad attempted to tell me he wanted to keep his relationship good with his son at any cost. When I suggested that not disciplining Steve at all left him with no father figure as well, Dad stated he thought Steve needed more love than discipline (my explaining that discipline was love did nothing to help).

Steve was now in our program after having been sent from the courts. When I suggested that his getting into legal trouble violated their contract (the contract that Dad had with Steve stated Steve would not get in any legal trouble due to drug usage), Dad assured me he did not want Steve to feel bad and that we should make the best of it.

On the unit Steve attempted many of his manipulations, most of which were quite futile. Having to follow the rules and be accountable was something Steve hated. He was angry with everyone for not allowing him to do as he pleased (as his father did). He actually told many staff (me included) that he hated us. His father had trained him to use this threat as a last resort because this is what his father feared most. To us, hating us was fine; he just needed to follow the program to remain here.

Steve became increasingly problematic on the unit and eventually he tried to smuggle drugs into the unit. This could not be tolerated and resulted in our expelling Steve from the program (and suggesting a much more restrictive program). Three days later Steve stopped by to pick up a few items he had left behind. When I helped him bring these things to his car, I was shocked to see a brand new red truck. When I asked Steve whose truck this was, he said, "My dad bought it for me the day you guys kicked me out. He thought I needed something to cheer me up".

His friend (Dad) did not think he needed to be disciplined for being kicked out of the program; he thought he needed a new truck. That would surely make things better.

The epilogue to this story was not good. A year later the dad called for advice. Steve had wrapped his truck around a pole in a drug induced state (with many drugs in the car ready for sale) and was now in a hospital with severe injuries, waiting for the police to charge him with a slew of offenses.

What could I say? It was obvious that Steve still needed a dad, not another buddy.

REVIEW

1. Being a parent is a unique and extremely powerful role. You will have many friends throughout your life but there will be scant few people who address you as Mom and Dad. It is an honor. Take it seriously.

2. It is important to remind yourself that although there can be times when you are a friend to your child; your main role is to be a parent.

3. When the parent/child relationship mutates into a buddy relationship, a whole host of problems occur. The most significant problem is that your child loses the leadership and guidance of the one or two people who are most invested in his long-term success.

4. In adolescence, having a friend instead of a parent can be a crushing blow. The adolescent is much more likely to make costly missteps which can warp the direction of his life. In addition, he is likely to assume that all authority figures will react like you. Thus, he will make errors in environments where mistakes can be quite costly, i.e. school, court, peer, etc.

CHAPTER 4

THE KID'S DICTIONARY: TEACHING YOUR KIDS THE MEANINGS OF WORDS

This is a very easy concept if you just take a second and think about it. Kids do not know the definitions of words from the dictionary. They know the definitions by how people react to what is said in their environment. If you pass the salt to a young child every time he asks for ketchup, he will think the word ketchup means little white substance you put on food.

When parents react in a way, which warps the meaning of the word, their child will define the meaning of that word in that style.

Let's look at a real life example of a young man named Paul in my practice (I wish I had videotaped this session because the interaction was so illuminating).

Paul was a very cute 12 year-old boy whose mother brought him to see me because "he is driving me nuts". His mother explained that Paul was terrible at taking no for an answer and just persisted and persisted in bugging her to change her mind. She was fed up and wanted me to help HIM stop.

I interviewed both of them and I must say Paul seemed like a typical 12 year-old boy. In addition, during our session I told him 'no' a few times to check his response. When he challenged me slightly, I explained that a 'no' meant 'no' and to please stop asking me since it would interrupt our time together. He seemed to take this in stride.

I decided to meet with Mom and Paul together and this is how the conversation went:

Dr. Matt: So tell me what the problem is?

Mom: He just keeps badgering me. Every time I say no he just keeps asking. It is driving me crazy.

Dr. Matt: Well let's take an example and show me.

Mom: Well we have 5 things planned today and we cannot do them all so I would like to skip going to Target.

Dr. Matt: Well, tell Paul he cannot go to Target today - it will have to wait.

Mom (directed at Paul): Paul we cannot go to Target today.

Paul: Please, Mom.

Mom: No

Paul: Please.

Mom: I told you I have too much to do Paul.

Paul: You said we could go.

Mom (to Dr. Matt): Do you see what I mean?

Me: I do (turning to Paul) What do you think your Mom means when she says NO?

Paul: Ask Again!

    And there it was - the kid's dictionary. I asked why. Both Mom and he acknowledged that she would cave in about 75% of the time — WOW. She had trained him to keep asking when he heard no because it was quite probable that meant yes with just a few more pushes. You see, Paul was smart and he was right. He knew what the dictionary meant by no (and this is why he conformed with me), but his mom had taught him a variation on this word and he was bright enough to pick it up — Bravo Paul!

    The problem here was Mom's not teaching him what the word meant BY HER BEHAVIOR. It soon came out she felt guilty about her divorce from his dad and she did not want to take the time to be tough. It was up to her to teach Paul the new meaning of no which meant she had to be willing to take some heat from her 12 year-old.

This is even more obvious in adolescence when kids become extremely good at finding soft spots and exploiting them. They not only understand the kid's dictionary but that words mean different things with different people. Remember, YOU are the teacher, not the dictionary.

The problem with talking to kids and then reacting in this manner is you actually provide kids with arrows for their quiver. They will watch how different words affect you. Then they will use them for their own good when they can. This is why 'it's not fair' is so effective with some parents and ineffective with others. Kids size up which words will 'work' and then use them when they can. The last thing you want to do, as a parent of an adolescent, is give him more ammunition to use in an argument.

I love the parent who melts into tears when their 5 year-old says, "I hate you". Talk about reinforcement. The kid does not even come close to understanding what 'hate' means, he just knows this might work to soften you up or get you to react. Want your kid to yell, "You are blueberry pie"? Just melt down and give in each time he uses it and you will see it. It is the reaction that defines the word, not the technical meaning.

My last story on this topic comes from a 16 year-old named Maria. She was brought to my office after lying to her parents regarding her whereabouts for a weekend. The parents told her she would be "Grounded for the next month". I asked her how she felt about her grounding and she said "Fine". I suggested a month was a long time and she laughed. When I asked why she was laughing she said, "My parents just say that". "I will be out next weekend", she added. When she came in the next week I was not surprised to hear she had gone out over the weekend. She had correctly figured out that when her parents said, "You are grounded for a month", what they meant was you are grounded until next weekend. She was right not to fight it. She knew what the phrase really meant.

REVIEW

1. Children and adolescents do not come with a dictionary pre-planted in their minds. They learn to use words according to HOW their parents use them.

2. The same is true as they grow into adolescents. They will respond to words the way you have used them. This is one of the main reasons I say to parents "Say what you mean and mean what you say". If every time you say 'no', you change your answer if the adolescent begs, then 'no' means, 'keep begging'.

3. Parents are often frustrated by this reality. It is not until they examine their own behavior, and see how they have trained their child/adolescent that change can occur.

CHAPTER 5

LET'S TORTURE OURSELVES:

REPLAYING THE PAST TO HEAL OLD WOUNDS

Most people suffer setbacks throughout life. I know of no one who has not had some difficult times in life. When we do not process and come to grips with these times in our lives (and instead hide from them and bury them) they leave emotional scars on our psyches. These scars are referred to as wounds and often drive our behavior in unexpected ways. We can see people trying to work out old wounds by replaying the past events over and over in their current lives. This is a futile attempt to heal the wound by changing the outcome of the old event in their current lives. These behavioral cycles often interfere with one's own emotional health, and can cause parents to act in ways, which are not productive for their children.

Let's look at a common example of replaying the past in one's current life. A young girl grows up with an alcoholic father. It is too hard for her to address this so she buries it and just gets through her teenage life. When she gets out of her home (and is free of the alcoholic) she marries an alcoholic and the whole thing starts again. Don't feel bad for the girl. She is choosing to marry an alcoholic with her eyes wide open. But why? Well she was wounded in childhood and never could really deal with the pain so she stuffed it inside. Now, as an adult, she carries that wound with her and it affects most things she does. She has not sought treatment so the pain and motivation of the wound stay subconscious. When she spots Mr. Alcoholic, something in her decides that this is the time to heal the wound. She marries him because *she is going to make it work out this time;* thereby, exorcising the pain of her father's alcoholism. Guess what? It does not work. The wound remains whether the guy changes or not (and 99% of the time he does not). In fact, if he changes, she will probably be gone because the wound will still haunt her. Fixing someone else is not going to fix her. She is looking for an avenue to heal and she will replay the drama over and over until she gets exhausted, sees a therapist, or dies trying.

My favorite example of this was a young lady (Emily – age 28) whose life was virtually identical to the above story. She was divorced from her alcoholic husband by 28 with 1 child. She could not change him and would talk incessantly about the similarities between her father and her ex-husband (they had even become drinking buddies). We explored her need to heal from her own wounds, but she was unable to grasp the concept telling me she would not fall into that trap again.

She called me about two years later. She told me she had grown quite a bit and was involved with a man she would probably marry. She was in love and knew she had broken out of all her old trappings. "He barely drinks", she said with glee. "I told you I would not fall into that trap again". As we spoke more, she revealed he had only one shortcoming. He was a 2-3 day a week drug abuser - "but never around the children". It was incredible to hear her defend this as good behavior.

I heard a few years later she had divorced him because she had concluded he was a drug addict, and she could not get him to change. What a shame. Since she has not worked out this issue, I suspect I will hear more of the same in a few years.

This happens with adolescents too. I treated a wonderful 19 year-old (Tara) who could not get enough support and encouragement. In fact, if she was not told she was doing well, e.g., she is pretty, she is bright, etc., she would come out and ask those around her for this validation. She was literally addicted to external validation. It did not matter that she was an extremely high achiever, accepted at one of the finest institutions in California, had earned numerous awards in various events in which she had competed. What mattered was to be externally validated which eventually drove those close to her away. Can you imagine being asked 15 – 30 times a day "Do you think I am doing great"?

If you examine her life story, you can see where the wound appeared. She became an actress at a very young age (a venue where external validation is paramount), and was very afraid she would fail. Mom's praise was the only recognition, which kept her from going nuts with self doubt. She used this coping mechanism to quell her fears. That is cute at 8, but not so cute at 19. She was trying to make it better by upping the encouragement only to see boyfriends call her on it and Mom become sick of telling her she was doing well. By the way, this young lady was not a shrinking violet, nor was she depressed. She was extremely outgoing, personable and beautiful. The good news was that she worked hard in therapy and was able to see herself replaying this psychodrama of being a scared 8 year-old. She would remind herself of this and allow her adult self to make the decision to act 19. This was a very powerful skill for her. She soon came to realize she could control the coping mechanism rather than have it control her.

Lastly, I had a very high-ranking CEO in my practice. She was in command of countless people and more money than most people will ever see. Over the years she had done a few silly things that would appear to be incongruous with her stature in life. Even she admitted these things seemed foolish for someone at her level, with so much to lose. Upon inspection, though, she was very forthright about her growing up with little encouragement. In fact, her mother often neglected her and she developed a belief that she was not really worthy. Now she is faced with a life where everyone around her sees her as worthy. You know what that does for her wound? Nothing. She still looks for ways to sabotage herself so she can confirm that her wound is correct. I am happy to report she has a firm grasp on it, but up until we started working together I would have bet she would have continued to compromise herself until this wound was confirmed and she was removed from her position.

All these stories share a commonality. Each person is trying to come to grips with a wound from earlier in their life. Instead of examining the wound, they are trying to replay it in their current lives. What they do not know is that replaying it in the here and now will not cure the old wound. In fact, the defense mechanisms they employed in the past are no longer of use now. An analogy to describe this will probably help. Imagine a young person who is drowning. He finds a small dingy and jumps in (these are his defense mechanism which save his life). It is now years later and he has drifted onto shore. However, he does not trust he is on shore so he refuses to get out of his lifeboat. Others tell him it is safe, but this boat saved his life – so no way is he leaving it. It is hard for people to let go of beliefs which literally saved them. Helping them to understand that the boat saved him once, but now imprisons him, is the task at hand.

When you see repetitive, destructive behaviors, look a little deeper and you will probably find a wound, which is fueling them.

REVIEW

1. Old wounds are difficult to deal with. If we do not come to a firm understanding of them, they tend to warp our perceptions and judgments in ways we cannot anticipate.

2. It is our job to become conscious of these wounds, see how they are affecting our current behavior, and then DECIDE how we will act in life.

3. These wounds are most often exposed when we do something completely incongruous with how we see ourselves. Or we make the same repetitive, self-destructive mistake over and over.

4. Therapy is a wonderful place to take a look at how these wounds developed, how they may be affecting us, and what can be done to alter them.

CHAPTER 6

<u>WHAT RULES YOU? THINKING VS FEELING</u>

Did you know that research seems to confirm that just processing feelings has little to do with actual behavior? Sitting around talking about feelings all day is great, but it gives the impression these feelings are determinative of behavior. Imagine deciding to act on your feelings all the time. You might feel like throwing this book at the TV set. Would you do it? Of course not. You would tell yourself 'I better not because that will cost me money and I will lose the TV set' (or hopefully 'I love this book and would never part with it').

I am amazed when people tell me how they feel, as if that should exonerate their behavior. Ridiculous. I feel angry when someone cuts me off when I am driving. That does not in any way excuse my rage if I act upon it. Thinking is always more important than feeling.

One of the most powerful tools we have to control our behavior, and therefore, our actions, is thought. Without it we are just primitive animals relying on instinct and feelings to make decisions about actions. For example, I 'felt' like playing hockey today so how did I end up at work? I will tell you. I 'think' that working is the right thing to do. I find it fulfilling and I 'think' I have a responsibility to my patients. Therefore, I overrode my feeling regarding hockey and came to work. This is just one hundreds of examples of a person feeling like doing one thing and yet doing another. Is there really anyone out there who ever 'feels' like doing laundry? Yet it gets done because your actions follow your thoughts, not your feelings.

In adolescence, this is especially important because adolescents have not yet fully developed the frontal lobe regions where thinking has come to dominate actions. Often-times adolescents are impulsive and behave very foolishly. They will do things that if they had thought about, they would not have done. It is your job as a parent to help slow these impulses down. After all, there is no creature as dangerous on our planet as an adolescent male. Just looking at the crime statistics will tell you that.

If you look at children developmentally you see that we are all born quite primitive. Our behavior prior to age one is entirely impulsive and based on reacting to our environments – thoughts do not control anything. However, somewhere around one year of age we begin to develop self-control mechanisms (called executive functions), which wrest control of our behavior away from our impulses and move them toward our thoughts. These executive functions increase in strength as the child grows into adolescence. In fact, a 13 year-old who acts like an 8 year-old in terms of self-control will find himself getting in a lot of trouble with adults and losing a lot of friends. We expect teens to control their behavior with their thoughts using the executive functions in their frontal lobes. Because we develop these executive functions we are able to think instead of just react to our environments. Those adolescents still reacting, instead of thinking, are the ones likely to make serious mistakes and end up either in legal trouble and/or shunned by those who think better and thus control themselves. Self-control is defined by making good decisions in the face of an environment calling for another response. We all want our kids to say no to kids who are behaving foolishly. Thinking clearly and directing one's own behavior is a product of executive function development, and should be reinforced by all parents.

The entire subject regarding executive function development and self-control is a fascinating area. If this were a book on brain development and neuropsychological functioning, I would go into much greater depth here. However, it is a book aimed at helping parents to parent teens, so what is important here is to remember that teens will often attempt to explain their actions using their emotions as a guiding tool. It is your job as a parent to listen and understand your teen while teaching him that thinking is the best tool to use when making decisions.

So one of my tenets is I am interested in how you feel, but tell me about your thoughts and how they will lead to actions. I have a large sign in my office from Nike, which says 'Just Do It'. It does not say 'Just Feel it'.

When you teach adolescents to act more on their thoughts, inevitably they get better because emotions and feeling are the last thing you want to use to dictate behavior.

There is a place in therapy to examine your emotions, but there is a far more important place where we talk about thinking leading to actions. You want to slow down enough to let your thoughts (not your feelings) dominate your behavior.

REVIEW

1. We judge individuals (and this includes adolescents) by how they act. There has been a destructive movement in our culture which suggests we should always be fixated on how we feel, and that our feelings in some way justify our behavior. Nothing is further from the truth. The jails are filled with adults who felt one way, acted, and then were incarcerated.

2. It is important to teach adolescents to understand their feelings but to act on their thoughts. How we decide to act should be controlled using our thoughts, insights and judgments, not our emotional state.

3. Thinking clearly and directing one's own behavior is a product of executive function development and should be reinforced by parents.

4. Parents need to help adolescents slow their impulses down so that thinking can guide behavior rather than emotion.

CHAPTER 7

FIVE STRESSORS THAT WILL REALLY COST YOU

Stress is the biggest killer in our country. There is no doubt that almost every major disease has psychological stress as one of its contributors. Nothing breaks down the human body more efficiently than being under stress.

This is just as true for families. Stress in a family can lead to terrible fractures in its foundation. In fact, one of the top reasons for divorce is money worries. Translated it means – stressing over money.

Below are five items, which I have found, increase familial stress dramatically. These should be avoided at all costs for your own sake and the sake of your children.

NASTY DIVORCES

Believe it or not, divorce gets a bad rap. Whenever I hear someone say that divorce is terrible, or that divorce should be outlawed, I ask one simple question. You know many divorced couples. Which of them should be together instead of divorced? People who have been espousing the virtues of staying married under any circumstances suddenly fall quiet. It is hard to think of a couple you would force back together. This is an example that in theory staying married is a great idea; in practice it has numerous problems, which outweigh the good.

What is of much greater importance to children and adolescents isn't whether their parents are married or not, but how their parents treat each other. Parents who are hostile and disrespectful to each other create a climate of fear and anger in a home. For these families, divorce is a relief and it decreases stress in kids and the family. The notion of staying married for the kids is outdated and unhealthy. Kids know you are staying married for them, and if you are not kind to one another this adds another layer of stress on them.

When couples do get divorced, if they are respectful and positive to one another, children of divorce suffer far fewer ill effects. If there is continued animosity and negativity, then the children feel this and are scarred by it. This is why it is so important not to put your spouse down in front of your child. Your spouse will not be hurt, your child will be.

I am often faced with the following dilemma. A parent will call and say their 12 year-old does not want to go to the other parent's home. My response it that it is your job to make this not just OK, but important to your child (the only times when this is not true is when the other parent is abusive, a danger, has a drug problem, or has an untreated psychiatric problem). It is not a feather in your cap that your child does not want to go to the other parent's home. Usually when kids do this, they are reading your negativity and following your lead. Whether you are a mother or father, it is your responsibility to assure your child that the other parent loves him. Unfortunately, the less mature a person is, the harder this is and so again the child is placed in the middle and stress increases.

TEENAGE PARENTHOOD

I am writing this chapter assuming you are in your late 20's – 90's as you read this. If you are not, you were likely a teenage parent. There is nothing quite as costly to parent and child as being totally unprepared for each other. I have worked with teenagers my entire career and have yet to meet one who is ready to be a parent. The combination of patience, effort, and sacrifice necessary to be a good parent is just not developed in someone so young. Even adults who have planned their pregnancy and are raising a child or children are surprised by the amount of work it takes. The skills needed to help guide another human being are not formed in teenagers. Thus, most of the time these situations end up in an emotional disaster. The reason so many grandparents are raising their grandchildren is because it is so obvious that the biological parent is not yet capable of handling this responsibility.

A secondary disaster occurs here as well. Having children this young is a poverty maker. Rarely can you climb the ladder of success with a child hanging onto you. That child needs your devotion, not school and/or a career. Thus, not only is the parent emotionally immature, but also financially she has just cemented her position in the lower class (unless someone comes along who will help them financially).

ABSENT FATHERS

The subtitle here is no disrespect to mothers. The need for mothers is obvious. I add this section to stressors because when children grow up without a male influence, they often have a much harder life. Simply look at the crime statistics and review how many criminals come from homes where there is no father influence. The influence of a male father figure cannot be understated.

Children and adolescents seem to know at a genetic/primitive level not to antagonize adult males. In fact, adult males may actually harm you if you are not careful – as often happens in the mammalian kingdom. I read a fascinating article regarding a game reserve in Africa. In the reserve the elephants were killing the rhinos. This was not good for the rhinos or for business. When an animal expert was brought in, he immediately identified the problem. There were a group of male adolescent elephants killing rhinos and the only parent was an adult female. She was unable to instill enough guidance and order to quell this behavior. When a male adult elephant was added to the habitat, the killing immediately stopped as the pecking order was now clearly established and obvious to the adolescent males.

Adult males in the form of fathers can carry a lot of weight in balancing and maintaining calm in a household. Households without this guidance can undergo great stress. This can be maintained in a divorced house by having adequate father time and by making parental decisions together and disciplining together. If you are in a non-traditional family, look for a man in your child's life who is kind, stable, consistent and wants to help. Then adopt him as an 'uncle'.

Make sure whatever man you have in your child's life is supportive of the role of the mom as well. I recently had a father tell his adolescent in front of me, "Whatever you do at your mom's house, I will not discipline you for it at my house." He then turned to me and asked why I thought his son acted out so much with his mom. Wow!

A PSYCHIATRICALLY ILL PARENT

When I am out speaking to audiences I am sometimes asked what is the most difficult problem I encounter for kids. I rarely have to hesitate. It is a having a parent who is psychiatrically ill and not being treated. Nothing warps a child quite as much as the daily negativity and craziness of having a parent who is psychiatrically ill. It is hard enough for people to weather these individuals for small periods of time. Imagine having to live with one and be dependent on one for years. Over the years, I have had several adolescents who have grown up in these households. Some become burdened by this and are greatly affected, some develop coping techniques that get them through, and the truly lucky ones have parents who see their own distress and do something about it before it spoils the family. Bravo to them, they deserve all the credit in the world.

HOMEWORK

This is a pet peeve of mine and one which I have seen hurt families by revving up anxiety. There appears to be an innate need for families to thrust homework onto their kids as if doing it will make or break the child. This is simply not true. In our educational system there is a tendency to pile on homework. We seem to have lost focus of its function – to help kids better understand and assimilate material already taught. Too many families build nine months of their year around homework time which is unreasonable. In addition, too much homework makes kids lose their interest in learning. They begin to see learning as a boring, repetitive task, rather than an opportunity to actually learn new and exciting things. I have yet to see a single study correlating the amount of homework done with success in life. It just does not exist.

I sat on a Board of Education and I can tell you many school districts have passed resolutions limiting the amount of homework, which can be given to kids. These districts cite the need for less stressful and more enjoyable family time. I strongly urge parents to value this time as well. If you believe your children are being unfairly burdened with excessive homework, go to your PTA meetings and your Board of Education meetings and let them know. You will be surprised at how many people feel the same way.

In all my years practicing, I have never treated an adult who has said, "The one thing I wish I had done more of in my life was homework".

REVIEW

1. The desire to avoid stress is an evolutionarily wise one. When you look at individuals it is easy to see how stress causes problems. The same is true when you look at families. Stress erodes the fabric of families and can cause long-term, irreparable problems.

2. In this chapter, I have listed 5 causes of stress that families should be aware of. i.e., nasty divorces, teenage parenthood, fatherless homes, having a psychiatrically ill parent, and homework. Most of these are avoidable if families decide to work together.

3. Remember, you can do a lot to reduce stress in your families and it is well worth the sacrifice to do so.

CHAPTER 8

LOVING A CHILD INTO A HANDICAP

MARSHMALLOW MOM & POPSICLE DAD

I assume that all parents who take the time to bring their children and adolescents to my office love them. But as with any characteristic, if you do it too much it becomes a liability. When you love your child too much and it interferes with your training them for life, you have a problem. I call these parents MARSHMALLOW MOM (so soft and malleable) & POPSICLE DAD (will melt at the slightest hint of heat). They just do not want to hold their adolescent responsible because it is sooooo painful for the Marshmallow or Popsicle.

I received a call from a very nice mom who told me she needed to bring her son into therapy. She said he was not going to school, he hung out with his friends all day, he never cleaned up after himself and he basically partied in the jacuzzi from morning until night. She said this had been going for some time and she was fed up with it. Also she noted she was divorced and the biological dad might or might not join us. I set an appointment time.

In strode a 32 year-old man. He sat and waited in the lobby. Assuming this was the boy's dad, I greeted him and asked when his ex-wife would be joining us. He laughed and stated he was not the dad; he was the 'kid' she had been calling about! This is a true story. This was early in my career and I was flabbergasted. Since this time, I have learned to be less shocked by such behavior as this mom who loved her child into almost total incompetence.

When the mom arrived, I asked why she did not kick this freeloader out. She explained he would never be able to make it on his own, as he did not know how to make his own food, shop, or even do laundry. What??? He's 32, partying with 21 and 22 year olds at your home all day long. After she works, she comes home, cooks for him and cleans the house while he and his friends go out (after borrowing money from her).

I explained to the mom that her son was who he was, but that she had the real problem. It took little investigating to uncover that her son was a very bright student in his day, but an underachiever. Rather than discipline him she tried to 'understand' him. Rather than punish him or allow the school to, she 'defended' him, eventually pulling him from school and allowing him to take his GED. He wanted to take a year off and find himself. Funny, he did not find himself in either Europe or South America, but instead came back home where his mom pampered him and continued to 'love' him. As the years flowed by, his peers moved on. He was stuck at the emotional maturational age of a 20 year-old and hanging with the same age crowd who considered the mother's house a flophouse.

This went on for the past 12 years with him always 'going to get a job' or 'almost in school' but something always got in the way (never his fault by his mom's judgment).

I told the mom she had succeeded in creating, from a smart and nice young man, a totally incompetent loser whose chances of success were now severely limited. Due to her 'love', he was quite handicapped. Adding insult to injury, he was a charming man and insisted that he saw no reason to change. He was quite confident his mom would not ask him to leave, and he felt no need to defend his lifestyle, which he explained, "Was a lot of fun". I will say she had trained him well and he had learned beautifully.

While this is a true, and an extreme example, one can see this often in everyday life. Parents, who do not allow their children to falter, or to pay a price, but instead 'save' them from their own decisions over and over, create handicapped individuals. In fact, I see this far more with bright kids and overachievers than I do with less fortunate kids (whose parents do not have time to helicopter over them all day long).

When a child does not tie his shoe correctly and falls, he has learned far more than tying the shoe correctly. He now clearly sees the problem and feels the pain of this mistake. Both are important and useful learning tools for children. As I tell parents, helping a child make decisions such as how to tie a shoe at age 5 is the template for making decisions like whether to blow dope at age 15. Both are decisions, and I hope your child has experienced both positive and negative consequences from their early decisions before they get to the important ones.

The same goes for making your adolescent's life too easy. If you hand everything to him, he does not learn the value of working for possessions and opportunities. This inevitably leads adolescents to feel entitled and to not understand the value of what they have. I had a patient once on the adolescent unit whose name was Stan. He came from a very privileged family and had never worked for anything in his life. He was 16 and was buying large quantities of cocaine and snorting it through a Bic pen when he was caught. When he arrived on our unit, I had my normal talk with him. Included in this talk was the system of rewards we had as each person progressed through the program. I stated that when he made it to Level 5 (our highest level), among other things I would be taking him to lunch. After I said this, he said, "With all due respect Dr. Matt, I don't think you could afford the places I regularly eat lunch". I laughed and asked why he felt that way. He then proceeded to tell me he received an allowance of $100 per day from his parents (that's $3000/month). What kid needs $700 a week? Again, way too much reward for way too little effort. Are you surprised he used that money to get himself in trouble?

Let me end this chapter with a story from my own life and how my parents wholeheartedly understood this concept. I was an achiever in high school having performed quite well and played two sports. I had gained acceptance at the University of Notre Dame. However, having recently turned 18, I knew far more than any other living person on earth about life, and it was time to show off that side of me. In June, just after graduating, I informed my parents I would not be attending ND in the Fall and I would not be taking a very cool camp counselor job I had worked the last two years. That was for losers. Instead, I was going to be horse player. I had a lot of experience at Fort Erie racetrack and I was going to spend my summer picking winners, and then use the money I accumulated to follow the circuit. I let them know I would probably be quite successful and they should not plan on seeing too much of me.

My parents asked if they could think about this, and then let me know their thoughts the next day. The next day we sat down and I was happy to hear my parents say, "We think this is an excellent idea and we would like to help you in any way we can. Maybe we can make sure you get up in the morning, make you lunch, or anything else, just let us know. We only ask that you do not formally withdraw from Notre Dame just now while you give this a ride". It was obvious they had become much less foolish over the past year. They too could see my GENIUS.

So every day I went to the racetrack. I was good. I won about 10% of the time and lost about 90 %. At the end of July, I had blown through the $1400 I had managed to save over the past two years. At this point, I was broke, jobless and needed cash. I went to talk to my parents one night. They were outside cooking hamburgers on the grill when I stated that I was in a 'little' trouble. I needed an advance because I was broke. They did not flinch, they just kept cooking. I got louder – "can I borrow some money, I am broke"? They said that is fine, but they would not be giving me any money and wished me luck. When I asked why, they stated to me that pony players are always broke and down on their luck. Since this is the life I have chosen, I should get used to it. They suggested I go to the track the next day and BEG for money from other players. NO LECTURES, NO "I TOLD YOU SO", NO DISCUSSION. Just, we supported you in your decision, and good luck to you.

The next week I got a job in a steel factory where it was about 1000 degrees every day. The work was difficult, and I burned my hands daily to the extent I needed gloves at night. I saved up enough to make Notre Dame palatable the first year. What a wakeup call!

Imagine how much I learned in this 2-month period. Did you think my parents knew I was going to get crushed? OF COURSE THEY KNEW. They not only allowed it; they supported it. They wanted me to see the power of my decisions and how the consequences would affect me, not them. They were comfortable with me being broke, jobless, etc. I was not.

These lessons are more powerful than 100 lectures or 10,000 books (with the exception of this one). This happened to me because of my own foolishness and I will never forget it.

Be like my parents, allow your kids to learn.

One caveat: I am often asked how far a parent should go? It is certainly OK to do what my parents did. I was in a secure environment, they knew what I was doing, and the loss would only be to my wallet and foolish pride. However, if I came home and said I was going to Mexico to sell drugs for the summer, obviously it would not have been OK for my parents to agree. Allowing your kid to learn from their foolish decisions, when the stakes are relatively minor, is important. What you don't want is to protect them so much from their decisions that they learn by being penalized when the stakes are high, i.e., being expelled from college, spending time in jail, losing a marriage, losing a job, etc. This is when losing some money on the ponies seems like a cheap lesson.

LEARNING TO FAIL

I see this a lot with the parents of high achieving adolescents. The parents have been clearing so much brush from the road that the adolescent has gone through life virtually unscathed, and therefore untested. These kids often do extremely well early in life. However, they become quite unsettled at the slightest speed bump in their way. If the path ahead is not clear, many of them recede because they have not had to deal with difficulty in the past. What is even more alarming is the fear they have of failure. It truly is the fear of the unknown because they have not yet experienced it in their lives. Quite the opposite of making their kids more competent, this kind of parenting robs adolescents of the life tests, which build the skills they will need as they mature.

Early in my career I had two parents bring their daughter to the hospital. They told me she had attempted suicide the night before. When she came in, she was a very cute 16 year-old. I told her what her parents had told me, and I asked what she had done. She then pulled her turtleneck down where there was an obvious and deep rope burn on her neck. She stated her parents had heard the chair fall and came in and got her. I suggested she must have been in terrible emotional pain to have attempted to kill herself. She said she was. "I learned yesterday I was going to get the first B I have ever gotten in a course – my life is over". It would have been nice if she had experienced some small failures earlier in her life to see that this was not the end of the world, but simply another opportunity to live and learn. We worked together for quite few months, and she eventually got the idea that her life was not about grades, but about handling life – both its ups and downs.

There is a prestigious university that knows this all too well. It is the kind of school where only a few apply and even fewer are admitted (or should I say 'are chosen'). The school knows this and on orientation day they bring all the freshmen together. They show the freshmen their schedule of classes and responsibilities. There is always a large gasp as it occurs to each one of them that this is virtually impossible. They are then told that although they are quite gifted, each student has one glaring flaw. "You do not know HOW to fail; consequently, you do not know HOW to get back up when you do", they are told. In life, it is not failure that ruins people; it is the inability to get back up and into the game. The freshmen are told they will have to make some real decisions this year including which courses and responsibilities to concentrate on and which to let go.

This will be reflected in their grades and reviews. Anyone not prioritizing will become overwhelmed and exhausted at trying to do everything. These freshmen are likely to be asked to leave. It will be up to each of them to decide in which endeavors they will fail. Then they will have to deal with that and move on. That is education at its highest level. The kind of education that does not just create smart individuals, but individuals who can prioritize in a time of crisis, make decisions about what is truly important, and accept responsibility in BOTH success and failure.

Lastly, as I have stated earlier I love to play hockey and it has brought me a lot of positives in my life. I currently take my 5 year-old son on the ice with me. He falls a lot. Initially, this seemed to concern him. I make sure every time he falls to let him know that falling is part of skating. I know he is really trying when he falls because he is extending himself, and that Daddy falls too when he is playing really hard. I let him know that his getting up is what makes him a player. Each time he struggles to his feet, I give him a high five and let him know I am proud of him for getting back up and going on. I tell him I do not ever want him to be afraid of falling. It is part of the game. Dealing with failures is what makes us stronger and less afraid.

REVIEW

1. The lessons in this chapter highlight the need for parents to truly consider what it is to love a child/adolescent.

2. If your definition of love means making sure your adolescent never has to learn the harder lessons in life, or accept the consequences for his behavior, then you will eventually raise someone who is incompetent and unable to get through life (and you will earn the title Marshmallow Mom or Popsicle Dad).

3. If your definition of love means to support your child/adolescent, while allowing them to learn valuable lessons from their own behavior, then your child/adolescent is likely to become a mature and well functioning human being.

4. Protecting your child from the consequences of his own behavior is one of the most self-centered and destructive things a parent can do. Not only do you rob the child of the ability to learn from their mistakes, you actually teach them there are no consequences for those mistakes and so no need to rectify them.

CHAPTER 9

STOP TALKING TO YOUR ADOLESCENT

I know this doesn't sound very psychological, but it is often true. Parents spend way, way, way too much time talking to adolescents about topics, which do not have to be discussed. It is imperative; if you are to be taken seriously, that when you discuss subjects with your adolescent they are subjects, which need to be discussed. Obviously, I believe you should speak with your adolescent. I just know you should be prudent and surgically strike when the time is right.

SAYING LESS IS MORE

When I entered Notre Dame at the age of 18, I loved the independence. I had gone to a college prep school, had very doting parents, and had grown up in the comfortable bubble of Buffalo NY. When I went to college, I did what a lot of other kids did; I blew off class and just had fun all day. I was not used to managing myself. Therefore, if people wanted to go out on a Tuesday night, I saw nothing wrong with coming in at 4 AM and sleeping through my classes the next day. About halfway through the semester, the Assistant Dean called me into his office. When I sat down he asked me how I liked ND. I said, "I love this place, I am having a ball". He said to me, "Well, I have your first round of grades and you are getting 4 F's and one D so you may not be enjoying it here much longer. In fact, if you do not get over a 1.0 you will be dismissed at quarter" (by the way I was a straight A student in high school). Now, believe it or not, this did not motivate me, but what happened next did.

I sat there thinking "Oh no, now I am going to have listen to some boring lecture from some guy about how I am blowing this opportunity". So I sat and waited, and waited and waited. After about a minute and a half (which felt like an hour) I said, "Do you want to talk to me about it"? He looked at me and said, "Mr. Duggan, I couldn't care less if you get your grades up or not, that's up to you, but could you please leave my office, I have another appointment." WHAT!!! He couldn't care less? Doesn't he know who I am? I am Matt Duggan! Isn't he supposed to care? Doesn't everyone care about what I do!

I remember walking down the stairs from his office and for one of the first times in my life thought: "I am really in trouble, I could get kicked out of here, and no one but me will really care". I went back to the dorm and worked my tail off and got a 1.8. I made it, but I was on probation. After that I became an excellent student and eventually earned a Ph.D. But that was one of the most powerful learning moments of my life, and I hearken back to it often. It was clear to me in that instant that there would be no encouraging, there would be no lectures, and there would be no effort by anyone to save me, except me.

Often I tell parents 'less is more'. Adolescents are much more likely to think about what parents say if they say less. The lecture series is over and is useless. Almost always adolescents know what you are going to say and can say it backwards. Repeating the same message has no effect, or actually has a negative effect by suggesting that you are the one who will change instead of your kid.

DON'T TELL KIDS WHAT THEY ALREADY KNOW

When I watch parents speak to adolescents in my office, I often interrupt abruptly. My usual question to the adolescent is, "Did you already know what your parent just said to you"? Almost universally the answer is "Yes". Then I say to the parents "Did you realize that your adolescent already knows what you just re-told him"? Again I get a "Yes". Then why are you telling him that? It's because parents want the adolescent to do what they already know, and the adolescent does not want to do it. This is not a time for discussion; it is a time for consequence.

Save your breath. Lecturing and haranguing them on stuff they know, only turns them off and tells them you are panicking. If you want to be an effective communicator with your adolescent, stick to messages that will be useful to them. Messages they do not know. I knew my grades were bad, but what I did not know was the Dean did not care if I was there or not. That information was significant and mind-boggling. The consequence was brutal – being kicked out of school. Telling your kids what they already know does nothing to cement your point; it only gives the adolescent another opportunity to fight with you.

Adolescents using drugs are often surprised when I ask them why they want to get off drugs. I tell them I need to hear because their getting off drugs is up to them, not me. It makes no difference to me if they shoot up or are clean. It needs to make a difference to them. I know the path, but I will not drag anyone down it. They must be willing to walk it. If not, let's not waste our time as I could use the session for someone who really wants to stop using. Immediately adolescents get that this experience is not going to be about cajoling, rooting, begging for them to stop. You would be amazed at the number of adolescents who see that session as a turning point for them.

I have a friend of mine who is a car dealer and very wise. He did not attend college, but has managed to do extremely well in a challenging profession. When he and I went to purchase a car, he said something to me I will never forget. We were negotiating that day with people who do this all the time. "Remember one thing", he said. "Often in a negotiation, the next one to talk loses". I pass this sage advice on to parents. Often talking is just burying yourself. Calmly state your point and then let your adolescent know the consequences and leave. Very powerful.

REVIEW

1. As a parent, I am well aware of the almost innate drive to talk and talk and talk at my child. This is counter-productive and actually teaches a child/adolescent to tune out at the first sound of your voice. It is important to state your point clearly and succinctly, if you want your adolescent to hear it.

2. Saying Less Means More – Most adolescents are desensitized to parent lectures. If truth be told, most of the time you are lecturing your adolescent, they are either day dreaming or conjuring up what they want to say next. They are rarely listening. If you say less, your adolescent will be caught off guard and actually consider the few, but powerful words, you say to them.

3. Don't Tell Adolescents What They Already Know – I do not think people at any age like this. When you do this, adolescents feel disrespected and as if you are treating them like a child. This approach usually just leads to further alienation.

4. Do have a discussion focused on asking them if they know why their behavior caused the current problem, and what they plan to do to keep it from happening again.

CHAPTER 10

IF YOU WANT PRIVACY & EQUAL RIGHTS– BUY A HOUSE

PRIVACY

This is one of those issues to which I have no sensitivity. Adolescents will come in and complain because their parents have "invaded their privacy". I do not even know what this is. "What privacy", I ask? "Well, you know, my room and Internet, and stuff", they say. I laugh out loud. Is this serious?

I tell parents, as soon as your adolescent owns his own house he can talk about privacy, until then what is in your home is yours – always. Given this, you can probably see what I think about snooping, etc. Do it - you are the parent. What happens in your home, you should know about. Is there anything more important than your child?– NO! Now I do not want to sound too draconian. I think there is a time to allow kids to develop a sense of ownership. That is, I do not think you should be on the phone listening to each conversation or run into their rooms without knocking. But if you think something is going on – investigate – your kid has no privacy that you do not grant him.

This goes double for the Internet. Whenever I have an adolescent who wants to get on facebook, etc. I tell parents that is good for them. Make sure you are a friend and you can look when you want. I tell this to the adolescent too. The moment you are removed as a friend, or the password is changed, the site is called and your adolescent's profile is removed. Imagine if I told you your 14 year-old can fly at the speed of light, get anywhere in the world, and create contact with virtually anyone. I think you would be pretty nervous and ask them not to use this power. This IS the Internet. It is your job as a parent to help your child negotiate this highway.

The same goes for blocks on your computer – do it. If you do not want your adolescent going to porn sites, block them. Same with histories. If the history is wiped out, your adolescent is wiped off the computer for a month. Believe me, they will not do this again. And this should not be a debate. The problem with most parents is they have become politically correct and listen to all this psychobabble on TV and radio. They buy into the notion they may be hurting their child's self-esteem by not letting them run wild. NONSENSE! Your job is to provide a safe, loving environment in which to teach your child how life works so they are prepared when they go out into the real world. Running amok under the guise of 'privacy' leads to a lot of problems.

VOTING RIGHTS

I received a call from a parent who wanted to bring her 13 year-old daughter into my office. She told me her child would not listen to her and would break things in the house. As we were speaking I was having trouble hearing over the racket in the background. I asked the mom what was going on. She told me she would not let her daughter go to her friend's house so she was breaking all the dishes in the house. I asked why she did not call the police. She said she thought it would hurt her daughter's self-esteem. She also noted that she did not want her child to go out and the child wanted to go so "it was a tie vote". We agreed to call the police.

When we finally met I encountered a much more subdued and demure young lady. The police had read her the riot act and done most of my work for me. They had told the mom (in front of the daughter) that this was her house and her rules would be followed. There would be no voting. The child could voice her opinion, which may or may not have any effect, but her voting days were over. This was not a shared democracy. The police suggested that if anything else was destroyed in the home, they would come out and incarcerate the girl. So much for equality. This case turned out to be extremely easy once the mom realized that kids do not have privacy or equal rights, they are kids. No adolescent should be burdened with the idea that they are running a household, and no parent should give up this right.

Harkening back to an earlier chapter, I am always surprised how easy this conversation goes. Why? Because kids know this and use it as a weapon, but when called on it, they let it go because they know it is vapid. Here's a fun sign from my office:

TEENAGERS: Tired Of Being Harassed
By Your Stupid Parents?

ACT NOW!! Move Out and Get A Job,
Pay Your Own Bills While You Still Know
Everything.

TRUST AND VERIFY

When I was running the adolescent inpatient drug unit, some adolescents would earn the right to go home on the weekend. Whenever that happened, I would call that adolescent into my office and inform him that he was getting a gift from me. He would be excited until he heard the gift was that I was going to drug test him on Monday morning when he returned. Invariably I would hear "Don't you trust me". My response would be "I may trust your heart, but behavior is sometimes very hard to control, even with all the tools we have given you. This is a gift from me to you because if all the other tools we have given you fail, you can always pull this out and inform people you will be caught Monday morning and thus cannot involve yourself with any drugs. Use this tool as often as you need to."

Most parents love their children and trust that they will do the right thing. It is not that the trust is misguided, it is just that adolescents sometimes need firmer boundaries to help guide their behavior. Therefore, I let parents know that it is OK to trust and verify with their adolescent if they believe he needs this help. Even though your adolescent will not like this, he is very likely to use this tool if he finds himself in a situation where he could get into a great deal of trouble.

One caveat here is that it is important not to make your home into a police state. Most of the time, your adolescent will not need this kind of boundary. For example, drug testing your child for the sake of drug testing is not a good idea. The adolescents I drug tested were one's already in an institution due to the quantity of drugs they were using. It is up to you as parents to know when your adolescent is placing himself in a situation where a firmer boundary will be useful.

REVIEW

1. I respect an adolescent who tries to convince his parents that he deserves to have his privacy respected, or he should have equal voting rights in the house. Respect, yes. Agree, no. There will be plenty of time for your son or daughter to have privacy and equal voting rights. That time will come when they move into their own home.

2. This is not to say you should pry into everything your adolescent does. Certainly common sense should reign here. For instance, if you are listening in on your adolescent's phone calls, you might want to look at what need is being fulfilled for you.

3. I think that parents should have a very good sense of what is going on with their adolescents. They should not be afraid to let that adolescent know that although they will be heard, the final 'vote' will remain with the parents, not the adolescent.

4. It is OK to trust and verify with your adolescent. Although he may balk at this, assure him you are giving him a tool to use to escape situations, which may not be in his best interest.

EPILOGUE

Most of the knowledge in this book has been gleaned from three important sources. First, from my own parents, siblings, wife and now my own kids. I have been blessed to be part of an extended family that truly believes that love is the foundation of any well functioning family. Second, I have been fortunate enough to have had supervisors and mentors who truly cared that I learned. Third, I have also learned from mentors I call patients. These children, adolescents, adults and families have welcomed me into their lives and shared with me their innermost thoughts, feelings, plans, ideas, etc. This trust, which has been bestowed upon me, is one I am humbled by and which I honor.

All of these people came here seeking help with one issue or another. I am glad I have been in the position to provide that guidance and help. As people leave my practice, they often reach out to shake my hand or hug me and thank me for my help. I hope they all know I feel the same way. Honored to have known them and worked with them.

This is a field where it is hard to 'fake it'. This goes doubly when working with children and adolescents who can tell a fake from a mile away. I hope that my sincere desire to be helpful and join them in their march forward has been evident. Joining them and helping them move forward can take many forms from talking, to supporting, to attending an event the client is proud of, to giving direct feedback, to giving homework assignments, to disciplining, etc. I hope all my clients know that whatever we used, we used it to make their lives better.

I have been a psychologist for almost 25 years. I have changed significantly due to the feedback and involvement with my clients. One motivation though that has never changed is my sincere desire to help make a difference in their lives. During these endeavors, each patient has left an impression on me, and I hope a little bit of me has gone with them.

Long Beach is a small town and I have been practicing here so long that I often run into current or former patients in the community. I am pleased that they feel free to come up to me and greet me. I love when children or adolescents run up to me and introduce their friends to me. It tells me that they do not see therapy as some 'world apart' experience, but as an opportunity for them to get something in a positive manner to better their lives. After all, we are all people trying to get by and I am glad they feel about me as I do about them.

I will finish by letting you know that I am often touched by the warmth and caring of my clients. Whether it is a smile, an invitation to a graduation party, a small note, etc., all these attempts to thank me are appreciated and remembered. After all, I believe that those of us, who are drawn to this field, engage in this line of work to make a positive difference. Money is a welcome by-product, but it has little to do with the gratification I feel by being invited into others' lives.

There are many, many moments I could recount that have provided me with that thrill of knowing a connection was made. Let me end by sharing one of those moments that I cherish greatly. A few years ago I received a call from a young lady who stated that I had treated her when she was 13 – 15. She asked if I remembered her, and I did. She stated she was now 30. She noted she was in a bad place back then and remembered how caring and comforting I had been to her and how we worked through some issues that helped her move forward. She stated she still reflects on many of those conversations and has often spoken of our discussions with her husband. She felt that our time together helped shape who she became. I was happy to hear from her and appreciative of her sharing all this with me. Then she said something that still affects me to this day. "My husband and I are about to have our second child. We know he is going to be a boy and we wondered if you would mind if we gave him the middle name Matthew after you?" Mind? It is one of the greatest honors ever bestowed upon me. I am honored that this person would think so highly of our time together.

While this is certainly a tremendous honor, this kind of situation, where a client is able and willing to share the benefits they have gotten from our time together, is why I really do this work. Seeing people grow into who they are to become, and be excited by their own prospects is exhilarating. This goes double when the patient is a child or adolescent. I think it is a cold therapist who can stand dispassionately by and not be moved by the efforts of his patients. I find I am moved on an almost daily basis by the courage and commitment people have to better themselves.

The path of affecting change goes both ways. While I have helped many, they in turn have helped shape who I have become - and I am better for it. So I would like to thank all of my patients for being so open and honest with me and for making it such a pleasure to work with them. These experiences have not only changed your lives, but mine as well.

Made in the USA
Charleston, SC
13 June 2012